Scripture Discussion Commentary 8

P9-DWJ-131

SCRIPTURE DISCUSSION COMMENTARY 8

Series editor: Laurence Bright

Luke

Luke	*Duncan Macpherson*
Acts	*Nicholas Lash*
1 Peter	*Bernard Robinson*

ACTA Foundation
Adult Catechetical Teaching Aids
Chicago, Illinois

First published 1971
ACTA Foundation (Adult Catechetical Teaching Aids),
4848 N. Clark Street, Chicago, Illinois 60640

© 1971 Duncan Macpherson, Nicholas Lash, Bernard Robinson

Nihil obstat : John M. T. Barton STD LSS *Censor*
Imprimatur : + Victor Guazzelli *Vicar General*
Westminster, 19 August 1971

2545

Library of Congress number 71–173033
ISBN 0 87946 007 5

Made and printed in Great Britain by
William Clowes & Sons, Limited
London, Beccles and Colchester

Contents

General Introduction

A few of the individual units which make up this series of biblical commentaries have already proved their worth issued as separate booklets. Together with many others they are now grouped together in a set of twelve volumes covering almost all the books of the old and new testaments—a few have been omitted as unsuitable to the general purpose of the series.

That purpose is primarily to promote discussion. This is how these commentaries differ from the others that exist. They do not cover all that could be said about the biblical text, but concentrate on the features most likely to get lively conversation going—those, for instance, with special relevance for later developments of thought, or for life in the church and world of today. For this reason passages of narrative are punctuated by sets of questions designed to get a group talking, though the text of scripture, helped by the remarks of the commentator, should have already done just that.

For the text is what matters. Individuals getting ready for a meeting, the group itself as it meets, should always have the bible centrally present, and use the commentary only as a tool. The bibliographies will help those wishing to dig deeper.

What kinds of group can expect to work in this way?

Absolutely any. The bible has the reputation of being difficult, and in some respects it is, but practice quickly clears up a lot of initial obstacles. So parish groups of any kind can and should be working on it. The groups needn't necessarily already exist, it is enough to have a few like-minded friends and to care sufficiently about finding out what the bible means. Nor need they be very large; one family could be quite enough. High schools (particularly in the senior year), colleges and universities are also obvious places for groups to form. If possible they should everywhere be ecumenical in composition: though all the authors are Roman catholics, there is nothing sectarian in their approach.

In each volume there are two to four or occasionally more studies of related biblical books. Each one is self-contained; it is neither necessary nor desirable to start at the beginning and plough steadily through. Take up, each time, what most interests you—there is very little in scripture that is actually dull! Since the commentaries are by different authors, you will discover differences of outlook, in itself a matter for discussion. Above all, remember that getting the right general approach to reading the bible is more important than answering any particular question about the text—and that this approach only comes with practice.

LAURENCE BRIGHT

Luke

Duncan Macpherson

Introduction to Luke-Acts

The authorship and date of Luke and Acts

There is no reference to the name of the author in either Luke or Acts, but there are strong reasons for supposing that if we can establish the name of the author of either of these books then we shall also have the name of the author of the other. Both Luke and Acts are dedicated to the mysterious 'Theophilus' (Lk 1:1–4 and Acts 1:1) and both works show many other similarities of vocabulary and style. The famous 'we passages' in Acts (16:10–17, 20:5–15, 21:1–18 and 27:1–28:16) all suggest that the author of Acts was a companion of Paul on his second and third missionary journeys. Obviously there could be other possible candidates for this post but the choice of Luke the physician, mentioned in Colossians 4:14 (see also Philem 24 and 2 Tim 4:11), is unanimously supported by all the ancient authorities and it is hard to imagine that they had any good reason to lie on this point as Luke was not a person of any particular importance.

The problem of fixing a date for the writing of Luke and Acts is a much more difficult one. The fact that Acts ends before the martyrdom of Paul would seem at first to mean that Acts was finished before the persecution by Nero in AD 64 but Luke clearly used Mark's gospel (usually dated around AD 65–66) and if Luke's gospel and

3

Acts are regarded as being written at the same time this would mean that Mark would have to be dated very early indeed. In addition to this problem we have to account for the way Luke fills out the details of the destruction of Jerusalem in his treatment of Mk 13 : 14 (Lk 21 : 20). Since the destruction of Jerusalem is dated AD 70 this suggests that Luke was writing about AD 75 and that he deliberately left out the martyrdom of Paul from his story. A plausible motive for this would not be difficult to find, as Luke is obviously very sensitive about saying anything which might upset the Romans and bring down more persecution on the church. Some scholars allege that Luke knew and in certain cases misunderstood the *Antiquities* of Josephus, which are usually reckoned to have been written around AD 94. This would mean dating Acts somewhere around AD 100, when Luke would have been absurdly old. The evidence that Luke knew Josephus' *Antiquities* cannot be regarded as completely conclusive, however. It is obviously very difficult to give an adequate account of all the aspects of this problem in short notes like these but a date somewhere around AD 75 would seem to have most to recommend it.

The special features of Luke's gospel

1. *Material peculiar to Luke*.

About half the material in Luke's gospel is found in Luke and nowhere else. The special interests and theological emphases of this material emerge quite clearly and the same interests and emphases are also apparent in his treatment of material taken from or shared with Matthew. If the author of Luke and Acts was, as seems certain, the companion of Paul, then this enables us to understand the reasons for the particular characteristics of Luke's version of the good news. Luke's gospel was written primarily for gentile christians drawn largely from the poor city dwellers of the Roman world. In every sense of the word these people were the outsiders. They were economically poor, of low social status, and had no share in the rich religious heritage of judaism. Luke's good news was precisely that these outsiders were the special recipients of the kingdom; the community of men under the rule of God which was to be brought in by the messiah.

The kingdom would reverse all the world's judgements on who was really poor and who was genuinely rich; an emphasis which the German marxist Karl Kautsky referred to as 'a savage class hatred against the rich . . . clearly apparent in the Gospel of St Luke' (*Foundations of Christianity*, 1908). Certainly poverty and riches are a distinct feature of Luke's gospel. Luke has twenty-one references to riches and rich men in his gospel, and all the references are disparaging. Mark has five such references and Matthew only one. Luke has eight references to poverty and the poor. Matthew has five and Mark four. Only Luke records the parable of the rich fool (12 : 13–21) and of the rich man and Lazarus (16 : 14 f). The three pieces of teaching on meals in Luke 14 firmly reject the class distinction which is the direct result of differing economic status. Zacchaeus, when he repents, immediately offers to recompense the poor (19 : 8). The pharisees, remote figures for many gentile christians, are characterised as 'lovers of money' (16 : 14). Only the truly poor can follow Christ and Luke places special emphasis upon the necessity of total renunciation of worldly goods in order to become a genuine disciple (14 : 28–33).

Only in Acts would Luke be able to give his account of how the gospel was brought to the gentiles but the ground is well prepared in his first book. All those who were of little or no account according to the standards of the official Jewish religion are represented as receiving a special invitation to the banquet of the kingdom. Samaritans, the heretics of the Jewish faith, are chosen as special heroes both in the parable of the good Samaritan (10:25–37) and in the story of the ten lepers, where only the Samaritan returns to give thanks (17:11–19). Both these items are peculiar to Luke. Publicans too were completely beyond the pale of official judaism, but were not beyond the scope of the kingdom. This idea is present in Matthew and Mark as well, but only Luke records the parable of the pharisee and the publican (18:9–18) and the incident of the conversion of Zacchaeus (19:1–10). Women, also, second class members both of gentile society and of the Jewish synagogue, receive special importance in Luke's narrative (8:1–3 and 24:10). But the kingdom is not offered to the social and religious outsiders in a purely arbitrary way. The kingdom is freely available to all; but only as a gift. The rich and the religious are not debarred by God from accepting the kingdom; they debar themselves by believing that it is theirs as of right. Samaritans, publicans, and other outsiders have no such illusions and in this respect they are like the gentile urban poor who constituted Luke's readership. Like Paul, Luke insists that it is only the acceptance of God's forgiveness as a complete gift that enables man to have any share at all in the messianic age.

The theme of repentance is a special feature of Luke's gospel. Only in Luke does Simon Peter begin his relationship with Jesus by confessing that he is a sinner (5:8). Only in Luke is the woman who anoints the feet of Jesus a repentant sinner (7:36–50). The exhortation to repentance in 13:1–17, the parables of forgiveness in 15:8–32, and the repentance of the thief on the cross (23:39–43) are all peculiar to Luke's gospel. Other characteristics include a much greater interest in the family of Herod Antipas; Herod himself is mentioned more times in Luke than in Matthew and Mark put together. Not surprisingly for the author of Acts, Luke gives far more importance to the role of the Holy Spirit, whom he mentions twelve times as against Matthew's six and Mark's three.

2. *Luke's use of Mark's gospel*

Of the 1149 verses in Luke's gospel about 350 are taken from Mark. 311 verses of Mark are either replaced by material from 'Q' (a document thought to have been used by both Matthew and Luke) or Luke's special source or else they are dropped altogether. Many of the omissions can be understood as part of Luke's sensitivity to the fact that he was writing for a gentile audience. Teaching which demanded a fair knowledge of the intricacies of judaism was omitted; for example the teaching about ritual purity and 'corban' in Mk 7 : 1–23; the discussion about whether John the Baptist was the prophesied second Elijah (Mk 9 : 9–13); and the more detailed discussion on the teaching of the law of Moses on divorce (Mk 10 : 1–12). The healing of the daughter of the Syrophoenician woman (Mk 10 : 1–12) is another incident omitted in Luke, perhaps on account of the apparent harshness of Jesus' attitude to a gentile.

Many alterations can be explained in terms of fitting Marcan material into Luke's different structure and time sequence. Details of place-names in Mark are frequently excised or changed. A number of passages in Mark have been cut out in favour of Luke's alternative accounts. The call of the first disciples in Mk 1 : 16–20 has been replaced by Luke's account which includes the miracle of the draught of fishes (Lk 5 : 1–11). Luke has his own account of the Beelzebul incident (Mk 3 : 22–30/Lk 11 : 14–23); the events in the synagogue at Nazareth (Mk 6 : 1–6/Lk 4 : 16–30); 'this generation seeking a sign' (Mk 8 : 11–13/Lk 11 : 29–32); sayings on causing scandal (Mk 9 : 42–48/Lk 17 : 1 f.) and the saying on salt (Mk 9 : 49/Lk 14 : 34 f). The discourse on love as the basis of the law (Mk 12 : 28–34) becomes an introduction to the parable of the good Samaritan (Lk 10 : 25–28).

If we look for convincing explanations for other omissions and changes there are many possibilities. Luke displays a tendency to attempt to tidy up anything that looks as though it could be a repetition. This might explain the omissions of the parable of the seed growing secretly (Mk 4 : 26–29) as too like the parable of the sower (Mk 4 : 1–20); Jesus walking on the water (Mk 6 : 45–52) as too like the rebuking of the tempest; the feeding of the 4,000 as a repetition of the feeding of the 5,000. Other omissions which might fall into this category are the anointing at Bethany (Mk 14 : 3–9), the first appearance before the Sanhedrin (Mk 14 : 55–64) and the wine mingled with myrrh (Mk 15 : 23).

Like Matthew, Luke tends to play down the failures of the apostles, and to suppress the glimpses that we find in Mark of Jesus' human personality. Mark tells us, for instance, that the disciples lacked understanding of Jesus' teaching (4 : 13, 9 : 10, and 9 : 33); that they criticised him (5 : 37), failed in their faith (4 : 38; 9 : 18) and that finally they all, without exception, abandoned him (14 : 50). Luke omits every one of these passages. Like the author of Matthew's gospel he was probably not closely acquainted with the twelve and he tended to regard them as something approaching plaster saints. The same exaggerated respect probably explains the removal of the passage recording the unworthy ambitions of James and

John (Mk 10:35–45) and its replacement with the much gentler Lk 22:24–27. Luke displays this same tendency in his treatment of the behaviour of the three apostles in Gethsemane (compare Mk 14:26, 32–42 with Lk 22:39–46). Members of Jesus' family tend to be idealised in the same way (eg in the treatment of the incident at the synagogue at Nazareth). In the case of our Lord Luke suppresses the information that Jesus spoke sternly (Mk 1:43); that he was thought by his family to have been beside himself (3:21); that he nursed children in his arms (Mk 9:36 and 10:16); that he felt an affinity for the rich young ruler; taught that the Son did not know when the last day would come (13:32); that he was bitterly confused in the garden of Gethsemane (14:33) and that he finally experienced complete emotional and spiritual breakdown on the cross (15:34).

3. *Material drawn from a common source with Matthew ('Q').*

Beside the material derived from Mark, or the material which is unique to Luke, there remain approximately another 235 verses thought to have derived from source 'Q', no longer extant. The name 'Q' is derived from the first letter of the German word *Quelle* meaning source. This source is thought to have consisted of a collection of sayings of Jesus. Whether it existed as one or more written documents or as an acknowledged oral tradition is not a matter of universal agreement among scholars but the symbol 'Q' is certainly a convenient shorthand for those verses where Matthew and Luke apparently agree to include material which Mark has omitted or given in entirely different form.

Here too we can see how the ethnic, cultural and class interests of Luke's readers can help us to account for some of the minor differences between the use which Luke has made of these verses and the use made by Matthew. Matthew was writing primarily for Jews; Luke for gentiles. Luke does not bother to mention that John is addressing pharisees and sadducees in his 'brood of vipers' speech (Lk 3:7–9 and Mt 3:7–10) or that it is the pharisees who accuse Jesus of casting out demons through the power of Beelzebul (Lk 11:15–16 and Mt 12:24–30). Presumably Luke's readers would not have been able to give very much meaning to this information. For the same reason discussions of the Jewish law are sometimes shortened, as in his treatment of the passage in Mt 23:1–36 (see Lk 11:37–54). Similarly it is possible to say that either Luke has accentuated or Matthew has softened some of the 'class hatred' in some of the sayings of Jesus. In Matthew it is not 'the poor' but 'the poor in spirit' who are to possess the kingdom (Mt 5:5/Lk 6:20); not 'the hungry' but those who 'hunger and thirst for righteousness' (Lk 6:21/Mt 5:6) and it is hard not to see a very marked change of tone as between Lk 12:33 f and Mt 6:19–21. In Luke Jesus invites his followers to practise a very literal poverty, in Matthew he seems to be asking his followers simply to practise inner detachment. It is just possible, of course, that Luke has changed the sense of the original sayings in order to please his readers but in the light of the way christians down the centuries have ignored or played down the teaching of the new testament on riches it seems much more likely that this tendency has already begun in Matthew's gospel.

Contemporary relevance of Luke and Acts

All these themes of Luke's gospel have tremendous contemporary relevance. Few people today can be ignorant of the scandalous contrast which exists as between the affluent developed nations and what is euphemistically called 'the developing world'. It is the opinion of some commentators, not least in the poor nations themselves, that this underdevelopment and poverty is a direct consequence of the economic realities in the developed countries. This is not, of course, the only social injustice which invites moral concern; racialism, poor housing conditions and underprivilege exist also in the prosperous developed societies. Concern about these and other issues have led to a more and more questioning attitude towards the materialistic assumptions of the consumer society, particularly among the young.

For all who share these moral concerns the radical perspective afforded by Luke's gospel will be especially refreshing. The central message running right through Luke is that where the gospel is concerned there are no outsiders. There are no limits either to the graciousness of God or to the real possibilities for human brotherhood. And that, after all, is what the word 'catholic' is all about.

Acts is a continuation of this theme in Luke's gospel. The style, structure and theological emphases of Acts all closely reflect those of Luke. Luke's gospel is the gospel of the outsider's share in the kingdom. Acts gives an account of how the message was brought to the gentiles. The extent to which this account can be taken to be historical; whether Luke used written or oral sources for his work; how far his record of events can be reconciled with the information in the letters of Saint Paul: all these are fascinating and difficult critical questions which are beyond the scope of short notes like these. Acts recounts how first the twelve, then the seven 'deacons', then Peter and finally Paul all initiate major missionary efforts. First the message is taken to the Jews in Jerusalem, then to the Greek-speaking Jews and the inhabitants of Judaea and Samaria, then to the gentiles of Syria and finally to the whole Roman world.

The all-inclusive character of the kingdom involved the early, Jewish, church in traumatic difficulties. To address the gospel to men of very different cultural background and historical experience involved them in a radical reappraisal of their own understanding of the faith. The analogy with the problems of twentieth century christians is obvious. Christians of all denominations share this painful, difficult and unavoidable task, but for Roman catholics in the years following the second Vatican council the analogy is particularly striking.

Book list

1. The articles on Luke and Acts in:

   (a) The *New Catholic Commentary* (London, 1969).
   (b) The *Jerome Biblical Commentary* (London, 1968).

2. Caird's *St Luke* (London, 1963) in the *Pelican Gospel Commentaries*.

3. E. J. Tinsley's commentary on Luke in the *Cambridge Bible Commentary* (Cambridge 1963).

4. W. Harrington's *Saint Luke's Gospel* (London 1968): a useful Roman catholic commentary.

5. A. R. C. Leaney's *A Commentary on the Gospel according to St Luke* (London 1958): an academic treatment of the subject which the serious student will find invaluable.

6. Earle Ellis' *The Gospel of Luke* (London 1968).

7. F. F. Bruce's *The Acts of the Apostles* (London 1951).

8. C. S. C. Williams' *The Acts of the Apostles* (London 1957).

9. Howard Marshall's *Luke, Historian and Theologian* (London 1970).

10. M. D. Goulder's *Type and History in Acts* (London 1964).

11. H. Conzelmann's *Theology of Saint Luke* (London 1960): the major work in this field for the more advanced student.

12. J. Dupont, *The Sources of Acts* (London 1964): the best introduction to the literary knots for anyone with the time and energy to attempt to unravel them.

13. A. Wickenhauser's *New Testament Introduction* (London 1958): useful for those wishing to follow up the critical questions in greater detail.

The sources of Luke's gospel

L: (peculiar to Luke)	Q: (material shared with Matthew)	Marcan material
3:1. Contemporary dates. 10–15. Preaching of John. 18–20. John and Herod. 23–38. Jesus descended from Adam.	3:2–9. Preaching of John. 16–21. John prophesies Jesus. 21–22. Baptism of Jesus.	3:21–22. Baptism of Jesus. (Mk 1:9–11)
	4:1–13. Temptation of Jesus. 13–16a. Jesus in Galilee.	4:16–30. Jesus at Nazareth. (Mk 6:1–6) 31–44. Jesus at Capernaum. (Mk 1:21–39)
5:1–11. The first disciples. Miracle of the shoal of fish.		5:1–6:12 follows Mk 2:1–3:14.
6:14–16. List of the twelve.	6:20–49. The sermon on the plain.	6:17–19. Crowds follow Jesus. (Mk 3:7–12)
7:11–17. Raising of the widow's son at Nain. 36–50. The woman 'who was a sinner' anoints Jesus' feet.	7:1–10. Healing of centurion's son. 18–35. The disciples of John.	

L: (peculiar to Luke)	Q: (sayings shared with Matthew)	Marcan material
8: 1–3. Women followers of Jesus.		8:4–15. Parable of the sower (adapted from Mk 4:1–20). 16–18. The lamp under a vessel. (Mk 4:21–25) 19–21. The mother and brothers of Jesus. (Mk 3:31–35) 22–25. Jesus rebukes the storm. (Mk 4:35–41) 26–29. Cure of the Gerasene demoniac. (Mk 5:1–20) 40–60. Jairus' daughter. (Mk 5:21–43)
9:51–56. The Samaritan village.	9:57–62. Demands of the apostolate.	9:1–9. Mission of twelve. Herod puzzled. (Mk 6:7–16) 10–17. Return of the twelve and feeding of 5,000. (Mk 6:30–44) 18–36 follows Mk 8:27–9:8. 37–50 follows Mk 9:14–50.
10:1. Mission of the seventy. 17–20. Return of the seventy. 25–37. Parable of the good Samaritan. 38–42. Martha and Mary.	10:2–16. Instructions on mission. 21–24. Thanksgiving of Jesus.	

L: (peculiar to Luke)	Q: (sayings shared with Matthew)	Marcan material
17:7–10. Unworthy servants.	17:1–6. Three sayings.	
11–19. Healing of the ten lepers.	20–37. The coming of the king-dom and the Son of Man.	
		18:15–34 follows Mk 10:13–34. 35–43 follows Mk 10:46–52.
18:1–8. The unjust judge.		
9–14. The pharisee and the publican.		
19:1–10. Zacchaeus.	19:11–27. The pounds. (no more Q sections)	19:28–40. Entry into Jerusalem. (Mk 11:1–11)
41–44. Lament over Jerusalem.		45–48. Jesus in the temple. (Mk 11:15–19)
		20:1–40 follows Mk 11:27–12:27. 20:41–21:24 follows Mk 12:35–13:20.
21:35–38. Watchfulness.		21:25–33. The coming of the Son of Man. (Mk 13:24–32)
		22:1–14 follows Mk 14:1–16.

All the remaining verses follow Luke's special source except for more or less direct use of Mark in the following verses: 22:18, 22, 42, 46f, 52–62, 69, 71 and 23:3, 22, 25f, 33, 34b, 38, 44–46, 52f, and 24:6.

1

The infancy narratives
Lk 1:1–2:52

Lk 1:1–4

The first four verses consist of a dedication, apparently made to a fairly important convert, perhaps a Roman official. Theophilus, however, means 'lover of God' so it is quite possible that Luke is writing to any and every convert whom he wishes to assist. The Acts of the Apostles begins in the same way and this fact is an important part of the evidence for supposing that Luke was the author of this gospel. The *many* compilers of earlier narratives must be taken to include both Mark and whatever source material Luke and Matthew shared (this material is usually called 'Q' after the German *Quelle*, source). 1:2 seems to indicate fairly clearly that the author of this gospel was not himself an eye-witness.

Lk 1:5–38. The annunciations

From 1:5 to the end of chapter two is apparently an independent composition. The style of the Greek is very different from the rest of the gospel and much resembles the style of the septuagint, the Greek version of the old testament. If the infancy narrative is taken as historically accurate then there might be some truth in the suggestion that Luke based these two chapters on discussions with

Mary herself, but the character of the work is much too
literary and contrived for us to suppose that the writer
is intending us to accept his story as literal history. Apart
from the names of Jesus, Mary and Joseph, the tradition
of the virgin birth, and the town of Bethlehem as the
birthplace of Jesus, with Nazareth as the scene of his
later childhood, the infancy narrative in Matthew is different in nearly every detail from Luke's account.
Neither writer is concerned with reporting the bare facts.
Both are trying to bring into relief different aspects of the
meaning of the birth of Christ. Both are very concerned
with showing how Jesus fulfils the old testament picture
of the messiah who was to come. The choice of this particular document to be included in this gospel may perhaps be due to one important similarity of emphasis with
the rest of the gospel. St Luke's gospel is perhaps most of
all the outsiders' gospel. The good news of the kingdom
of Christ reaches out to all those who were of little account and to those who seemed to be beyond the help of
the official religion of the time. That John should have
been born to a barren woman, the messiah born in a
stable, and shepherds become the first to honour him, all
fit in perfectly with this interest in the humble and the
rejected.

The section weaves together two annunciation stories.
In both stories we find an angel proclaiming an impending birth, in one case the birth of the messiah and in the
other of the forerunner of the messiah. Both events are
occasions for rejoicing and both are taking place in fulfilment of old testament prophecy. Both recipients of the
messages are astonished; Zechariah because of his own
age as well as his wife's and because of his wife's barrenness; Mary because she has not had sexual union with a
man. Luke's emphasis on the miraculous character of the

conceptions in both cases reinforces the idea already suggested by the presence of an angel, namely that the births
of the two babies will mark a new, dramatic, and mo-
mentous intervention by God into human history. Both
annunciations also have interesting parallels with the annunciation of Samson (Jgs 13:1 ff) and the events preceding the birth of Samuel (1 Sam 1).

In 1:5 Luke gives a careful account of the historical
setting for Zechariah's vision. Herod the great ruled not
just Judaea but all Palestine from 37–4 BC. The 'division
of Abijah' was the eighth of the twenty-four groups of
priests (1 Chron 24:10) who shared between them the
daily ritual of the temple. Sirach 50:12 f gives a description of the tasks involved in this morning act of worship.
Zechariah is terrified by the apparition of the angel who
prophesies the birth to Elizabeth of a child who is to be
the forerunner of the messiah, the new Elijah who would
warn Israel to repent (Mal 4:5). Like Isaac (Gen 16),
Jacob (Gen 25), Joseph (Gen 30), Samuel and Samson,
John is to be born of a barren mother and, like the Naza-
rites (Num 6:23, Jgs 13:4, and 1 Sam 1:11), his consecration to God will be marked by his abstinence from
alcohol.

The salutation given to Mary in 28–30 is based upon
Zeph 3:14–17, where the people are personified as
the 'daughter of Zion' who is exhorted to rejoice in confidence of victory since the Lord is within her. (The
translation 'Hail' in the catholic edition of the RSV is
merely a concession to catholic usage. 'Rejoice' conveys
the meaning of the Greek original much more closely).
Mary now becomes the 'daughter of Zion' and a representative figure for the people of God. Theologically
speaking, belief in the divinity of Christ is not dependent
upon the truth of the story of the virgin birth, nor should

belief in the virginal conception of Christ be interpreted as reflection on the wholesome character of the sexual act. Old testament writers like Hosea, Amos, Ezekiel and Jeremiah all spoke of Israel as an unchaste wife of Yahweh. Mary provides the symbol of the faithful remnant of the old Israel. That Jesus is born to her is a way of asserting his continuity with past history; that he had no human father is a way of asserting the freshness of God's initiative.

1. How far has a false understanding of Mary's virginity contributed to an unbalanced christian attitude towards sex?

2. In what ways has the role of Mary in the gospel contributed to the attitudes towards women in successive European cultures and civilisations?

Lk 1:39–56. The visitation and the Magnificat

The early church was very anxious to assert the close relationship between the mission of John the Baptist and the mission of Jesus, especially in view of the existence of followers of John who were not in fact christians (see Acts 19:1–7). Luke projects the Baptist's recognition of Jesus right back to his existence in the womb. If the event had any historical basis, then it would have been Elizabeth who was aware of this and hardly her child. Elizabeth greets Mary in language reminiscent of the way in which the people praised Judith after she had assassinated Holofernes (Judith 13:18). Some Roman catholic scholars see a striking similarity between the language used by Elizabeth in greeting Mary and the language used by David in greeting the ark (2 Sam 6:9). Those who follow this line of thought see further parallels in the *Magnificat* which follows. If this hypothesis is correct then the author is proclaiming Mary as the new ark of the covenant in which the glorious presence of Yahweh is contained. Certainly the symbolism of Mary as the ark is very old but this interpretation remains only hypothetical.

The *Magnificat* is so very like the song of Hannah (1 Sam 2:1–10) that a small minority of ancient manuscripts have put it in the mouth of Elizabeth rather than Mary, as it is Elizabeth and not Mary who, like Hannah, is an old and previously barren woman who has been enabled to conceive by God. It is of course unlikely that the *Magnificat* was actually composed by either Mary or Elizabeth and it is probably based on a number of psalms and canticles, some of which are no longer in existence. The song has a strong revolutionary flavour: God has lifted up the poor and impoverished the rich, and structures of oppression have been turned on their heads. If we imagine a song rather like the *Magnificat* being chanted by a group of Jewish guerillas returning from a successful raid on the Macedonians during the Maccabean revolt, we will get something of the real flavour of this type of composition. God's vindication of Mary's humility is seen in the same kind of terms and Mary is seen as a representative figure for the whole people of God.

In what ways might a greater emphasis on Mary's symbolic importance as the personification of the people of God make catholic devotion to Mary more acceptable to protestant christians?

Lk 1:57–2:20. The births of John the Baptist and Jesus

The account of the birth of John follows as well as Zechariah's song of thanksgiving, the *Benedictus*. The

Benedictus is in many ways very like the *Magnificat* and most of the verses have clear echoes in the psalms. Verses 75–79 underline the christian understanding of John's vocation as the forerunner of the messiah. Verse 80 has been interpreted by some scholars as meaning that John was adopted by the Essene sect. Essenes were communities of ascetics living in the desert waiting for the coming of the messiah. The account of the birth of Christ begins with historical references which are intended to indicate roughly the time when Jesus was born—Augustus reigned from 30 BC–AD 14—but we have no entirely clear corroborating evidence for a world-wide census, which included Palestine, taking place. Joseph may have had some family connections that compelled him to register at Bethlehem.

The birth of Christ is represented as taking place in acutely impoverished conditions. It is hard not to see something profoundly symbolic in this episode, written perhaps in the light of Paul's understanding of the incarnation (2 Cor 8:9). The angels appearing to the shepherds perform the same function as the angel appearing to Mary and Zechariah. Angels are a way of asserting God's decisive intervention and presence in history. The image of '*the glory of the Lord*' (2:9) reinforces this idea. The glory of the Lord, frequently associated with a cloud, is a very old symbol for God's point of encounter with man, going back to Moses' encounter with God in the cloud on Sinai. Originally, perhaps, the idea owes something to primitive man's discovery that he could look at the glory of the sun's rays when their light was filtered through a cloud.

The poverty of the shepherds again underlines the revolutionary character of the birth of Christ. Born in poverty, his message is the message of liberation and joy for the poor.

How far does the festival of Christmas help to obscure the real meaning of the birth of Christ? Do you think that it is true that even the churches help to sentiment- alise this event?

Lk 2:21–40. The circumcision and presentation of Jesus

The circumcision of Jesus, which included the naming ceremony, completes the parallel between the birth of Jesus and the birth of John. Circumcision was a legal requirement of the Jewish law (Lev 12:3), as were the ritual purification of the mother (Lev 12:2, 4) and the consecration of the first-born son (Ex 13:2, 12). By sub- mitting to these requirements of the law Jesus recapitu- lates the history of Israel and expresses his solidarity with the Jewish people. Jesus is 'born under the law' (Gal 4 : 4). The recognition of Jesus as messiah by the priest Simeon and the prophetess Anna both emphasise the idea that the consecration of the messiah is seen as mark- ing the beginning of the new age, the age of the messiah. Simeon's prophecy in verses 32–35 again reflects the influence of the psalms, his song, the *Nunc Dimittis*, brings out the longed-for character of the coming of the messiah, and his prophecy emphasises the decisive char- acter of God's intervention; so decisive that everybody has to decide which side they are on because the messiah is a disruptive influence, 'a sign that is spoken against', and 'the thoughts out of many hearts' are going to be re- vealed. Decision whether they are on the side of God's revolution or against it will make for 'the fall and rising of many in Israel'.

2 : 40 parallels 1 : 80, where, as we saw, John the Baptist 'grew and became strong in spirit'. 2 : 40 tells us that Jesus 'grew and became filled with wisdom; and the favour of God was upon him'.

Should the church expect success? In what terms?

Lk 2:41–51. The episode of the finding in the temple

This passage re-emphasises Jesus' submission to the law. Luke gives us this account of Jesus going up to the temple for the major feasts from the age of twelve, the age of puberty, onwards. The chief point of the story seems to be in verse 49, 'did you not know I must be in my Father's house' (or otherwise, 'I must be about my Father's business'). Here Jesus gives absolute priority to his mission as the son of the Father over every other consideration, including even a consideration of family loyalty. It is difficult not to read something more than mere biographical record into the three days in which Mary spent seeking for him, when we remember that Jesus' followers were seeking Jesus sorrowing and on the third day they encountered him risen from the dead. 2 : 51, 'and he went down with them and came to Nazareth and he was obedient to them' contrasts notably with the interesting accounts of the childhood of Jesus which are given in some apocryphal gospels and with the popular importance given to the childhood of Christ and the holy house of Nazareth in catholic piety. The evangelist did not think that biographical details were in themselves important unless they helped to bring out more vividly the character of Christ's mission.

1. Does devotion to Jesus as a child or to the holy family of Nazareth necessarily detract from a balanced christian understanding of Christ?

2. Does the holy family really provide a helpful model for christian family life? Can you suggest any points of similarity at all between the holy family and the average christian family today?

2

Prelude to the public ministry of Jesus Lk 3:1–4:13

Lk 3:1–18. The preaching of John and the baptism of Jesus (Mk 1:1–11; Mt 3:1–17)

It must be remembered that the Jewish people at the time of the ministry of John the Baptist had more than one concept of the kingdom. They all had in common the idea that the kingdom would represent God's liberation of man from bondage. At least one strand of the idea consisted of a notion of nationalistic political liberation; that God would raise up a military leader who would drive out the Romans. Other ideas current at the time involved much more in the nature of a cataclysmic divine revelation, the destruction of the present world order and the rule of God himself through his messiah from Jerusalem. Other ideas of the kingdom included the idea of the kingdom as primarily an interior and a moral kingdom.

Without specifying the exact character of the kingdom, John invites his hearers to repent in the face of the imminent coming of the messiah. In the beginning of Lk 3:1–2, we see a clear indication of the start of a fresh document. Again we see the date being indicated with a lot of cross-references: Tiberius reigned AD 14–37, Pilate's dates have been calculated as AD 27–37, Herod Antipas 4 BC–AD 39; Philip 4 BC to AD 34; Annas AD 7–14 and Caiaphas AD 18–36.

'The word of God came to John' puts John in the role
of a prophet. Since these words are only found in Luke,
and Luke fails to mention John's bizarre life-style and
costume, some scholars have suggested that Luke is anxious to play down the idea of John as a new Elijah. John
was preaching the baptism of repentance, and baptism
was already known in judaism, particularly as a way of
initiating gentile converts to judaism. Baptism here is an
outward sign of an internal repentance. The quotations
from Is 40 : 3–5, and the clear echoes of Is 49 : 11,
42 : 16 and 45 : 2 and Zech 4 : 7 all combine to bring
out the decisive and revolutionary character of the
coming of the messiah; the mountains and the hills
being brought low and the crooked becoming straight
are powerful symbols of radical change. In the face
of this John invites his listeners, not specified as they
are in Matthew, to bring forth fruit worthy of repentance. Repentance involves radical renewal, a complete
change in values and priorities and represents more
than mere remorse over misdeeds, and that is why John
insists upon fruits of repentance. 'Do not begin to say to
yourselves that we have Abraham as our father'; the
point that John is making here is that repentance is impossible to those who trust in the privileged character of
their religious and national heritage. It is only the fruit
that is decisive; that indicates the value of the tree. Luke
is alone in telling us of specific advice to the publicans
and to soldiers. In both cases the advice he gives is little
less than impossible; for publicans not to extort, when
this was the only way in which they were able to make a
living, and to ask soldiers not to do violence, is asking
the impossible, but in the face of the coming revolution the impossible is no less than is asked for. God's

intervention represents a judgement upon those who do
not repent; 'he will gather the wheat into his granary but
the chaff he will burn with unquenchable fire'. 3:16, together with the incident of the baptism of Jesus, which is
also taken from Mark, both emphasise the subordinate
character of John's ministry in relation to that of Jesus.
Jordan itself is a symbol of the new age. When the Israelites first entered into the promised land they had to cross
over the river Jordan. Jesus is baptised. Baptism is a
symbolic death often employed in the initiation of gentile converts to judaism. The baptism of Jesus, then,
anticipates his crucifixion and is represented as the occasion upon which he committed himself totally and publicly to his messianic mission. The voice and the descent
of the dove are seen as an expression of divine approval
of Jesus' act of commitment.

Only Luke adds that the dove 'descended upon him in
bodily form' and some scholars have taken this as an emphasis upon the objective character of the vision, but this
may well be to read too much into the words. The dove
represents the Spirit of God who 'was moving over the
face of the waters' at the dawn of creation (Gen 1:2).
Some ancient authorities complete the quotation 'Thou
are my beloved Son' with the words 'this day I have be-
gotten thee' (see Ps 2:7). If this was the earlier form of
the text then it is easy to see why it was changed, as some
followers of the adoptionist heresy held that Jesus only became God's Son at his baptism, and this reading could
be held to support their position.

*1. Does christianity make impossible demands? To
what extent would a more realistic approach be preferable?*

2. *Do you agree that the new testament idea of repentance has been debased in much popular piety? How does this happen and why?*

Lk 3:23–38. Jesus' descent from Adam

Much importance was placed on genealogies in the ancient world. Unlike Matthew's genealogy, which represents Jesus as descended from Abraham and David, the Lucan genealogy is concerned with showing Jesus' descent from Adam. Jesus fulfils the history of the whole human race. Only fourteen of the names in this list are the same as the names in the genealogy in Matthew and this should help us to see that the only important point here is that Jesus fulfils all human history. We should not attempt to take this genealogy literally as an account of Jesus' ancestry.

Some scholars claim that they can discern two traditions about the conception of Jesus in Luke; one tradition supports belief in the virginal conception of Jesus, the other, older, tradition, assumes that Joseph was Jesus' father. This genealogy, showing Jesus' descent through his father's line, is taken as part of this earlier tradition. In the ancient world, however, adoption was sufficient ground for legal inheritance. The Emperor Augustus, for instance, was the adopted son of Julius Caesar. Unfortunately it is a notorious fact that both defenders and opponents of belief in the virgin birth too often rival each other in prejudice and partiality when it comes to this question. Whether Jesus could or could not have been born without a human father or whether the catholic church teaches this as a fact, in neither case can we determine in advance how the highly problematical evidence of the new testament is to be interpreted.

Can you suggest any reasons why some people might find it difficult to approach a topic like the virgin birth without becoming extremely partisan about the evidence?

Lk 4:1–13. Jesus is tempted in the wilderness

Luke here develops the very brief account of the temptation of Jesus in Mark 1 : 12–13. Most of his material is shared with Matthew (4 : 1–11) although Matthew has the second and third temptations in the reverse order from Luke. In 4 : 5 Luke does not mention that Jesus was taken up onto 'a very high mountain' (Mt 4 : 8) and the words 'in a moment of time' are peculiar to Luke's account. Only Luke includes the devil's explicit claim to have authority over the kingdoms of the world (4 : 6).

Like Moses and Elijah Jesus fasts for a period of forty days. Moses had fasted forty days before receiving the ten commandments (Ex 34 : 28) and Elijah fasted for forty days in 1 Kgs 19 : 8. The term 'forty days' was not used as an exact term in biblical times but was a very general description of a period of five or six weeks. It is also possible to see a parallel between the forty days Jesus spends preparing for his public ministry and the forty years spent by the Israelites in the desert in preparation for their entry into the promised land. Jesus is summing up in his own person the law (Moses); the prophets (Elijah) and indeed the entire history of the Jewish people in their exodus experience. Unlike the Israelites he does not tempt God by seeking to obtain bread in the desert. Unlike the Israelites who worship the golden calf, he refuses to bow down and worship Satan and he refuses to tempt God by doubting God's sustaining power and love. Satan himself should not be seen as the fallen angel of later theology but rather as the symbol of man's ambiguous relationship with God. He is the accuser who stands before the throne of God putting man in bad conscience in God's presence. He is the symbol of man's estrangement from himself and from the world in which he finds himself. Irenaeus thought of the moment when Jesus refused to give in to the devil's temptations as the fall of the devil. Not until Jesus turned the devil away did the devil lose his place as an agent of God.

1. Is the devil just a part of the furniture of the new testament world or is it impossible to understand the new testament without retaining belief in the devil?

2. Do the kingdoms of the world really belong to Satan and are political power-structures part of man's estrangement?

3

Jesus' ministry in Galilee
Lk 4:14–9:50

This section is largely based on Mk 1:14–9:41, and groups together twenty-four acts of Jesus. Apart from Mk 6:45–8:26 all the Marcan material is included and only Luke 5:1–11 and 6:12–8:3 are drawn from sources outside Mark's gospel.

Lk 4:14–15. Introductory verses (Mt 1:14 and Mt 4:12)

These two verses summarise the section which is to follow. In Mark's gospel the entry of Jesus into Galilee is linked with the arrest of John, so that Jesus' work is seen as being in some way continuous with the work John has been obliged to abandon. Luke puts the emphasis instead upon the work of Jesus as being impelled by the Spirit—a characteristic change as Luke always gives particularly strong emphasis to the role of the Spirit.

Lk 4:16–30. Jesus in the synagogue at Nazareth (Mk 6:1–6 and Mt 13:53–58)

It was quite usual for the president of the synagogue to invite respected members of the congregation to expound a text and these verses do not necessarily answer the question of whether Jesus was a trained rabbi. Only

Luke shows us Jesus taking the text of Is 61 : 1–2 and turn-
ing it into the manifesto for his kingdom. It is Jesus himself who has been anointed at his baptism to proclaim
the good news of liberation to the poor. The commentary
he offers is brief but to the point (4:21): 'Today this
scripture has been fulfilled in your hearing'. Jesus is asserting that the kingdom has come in his own person.
But in Nazareth at least the gospel of liberation is not
believed; familiarity has bred contempt and Jesus responds to their unbelief by attacking their religious self-
assurance. The good news will only be for the poor, for
the outsider, for those who have no reason to be self-
assured. Jesus uses the old testament to reinforce his
point. Elijah was not sent to an Israelite woman (1 Kgs
17 : 9 f.) and Elisha did not heal an Israelite leper (2 Kgs
5) but a Syrian. In both cases it was complete outsiders,
gentiles, who were the recipients of God's mercy. Luke
has quite deliberately placed this incident at the beginning of Jesus' ministry in order to set the tone for the
whole of Luke and Acts, showing that Jesus was rejected
by the institutions of the Jewish religion so the message
was preached to the gentiles. Comparison between Luke's
account of the incident and the accounts to be found in
Matthew and Mark show how Luke has changed the basic
point of the story for precisely this reason. In Mark Jesus
is rejected 'among his own kin and in his own house' (Mk
6 : 5). Matthew is sensitive about the possibility of seem-
ing to disparage Jesus' own family circle but there is no
attempt to give the episode the wider significance which
Luke has given it.

*Does the confidence derived from being a practising
member of a religion necessarily prove to be a hindrance
when it comes to accepting the kingdom?*

Lk 4:31–44. Miracles at Capernaum (Mk 1:21–39 and Mt 4:23–25, 7:28f. and 8:14–17)

Each of Jesus' miracles should be seen as a sign that the kingdom had come in his own person. According to popular mythology mental illness was attributable to possession by evil spirits. The coming of Jesus' kingdom means that these evil spirits no longer have any power. The question 'Have you come to destroy us?' (4:34) does not require a verbal response. Jesus' action demonstrates that this is precisely part of his mission.

With our modern understanding of mental illness is it still possible to give any meaning to the exorcisms of Jesus?

Lk 5:1–11. The calling of the first four disciples (Mk 1:16–20 and Mt 4:18–22)

The miraculous episode of the draught of fishes is found only in Luke, although it is very like the resurrection appearance in Jn 21:1–6. Comparison of this text with Mark's and Matthew's accounts will also show that Luke is giving special prominence to Peter as the spokesman of the apostles, perhaps in anticipation of the role he will play in the first fifteen chapters of Acts. The overflowing net is frequently used as a symbol for the coming kingdom. Peter's future work will be to help Jesus bring in the harvest, not this time of fish but of human beings. Only in Luke do we find the term 'Gennesaret' being used to denote the sea of Galilee. In Mark and Matthew it is used to denote the geographical region around Galilee.

Would it be more appropriate for bishops in the church today to think of themselves as fishermen or, in the other biblical image, as shepherds?

Lk 5:12 to 26. Two miracles of healing (Mk 1:40–2:12 and Mt 8:1–4 and 9:1–8)

In these verses Luke returns to Mark's narrative and follows it fairly closely although Luke situates one episode in an unspecified town. The leper, who is a complete outsider to the Jewish religious cult because of his ritual uncleanness, is cleansed by Christ and, in accordance with the instructions in Lev 14 : 2–32, he goes to the priests for them to certify that he has recovered from the disease. As in other miracles of Christ, the person who is cured in many ways represents everybody who is restored to wholeness through the mission of Christ. In verses 17–26 we find the miracle of the palsied man lowered through the roof. To understand this miracle it is important to realise that the Jews at the time believed in immanent justice, that is to say, that one's fortunes and misfortunes in this life were a direct consequence of one's faithfulness or lack of faithfulness to God. To be possessed by a demon might signify only bad luck, but sickness was usually taken to be a chastisement for personal sin. Though Jesus denies this proposition in Matthew and John, here he takes it for granted and uses the idea that his messiahship includes his sharing in Yahweh's prerogative to forgive sin. Those who refuse to credit that he can forgive sins are invited to see the results of his action: 5 : 24 'but that you may know that the Son of man has authority on earth to forgive sins'. Only Luke adds the unlikely detail that the man was lowered 'through the tiles'. The flat roof implied in Mark's account sounds much more plausible.

Is it possible to maintain that personal misfortune, illness for example, is a consequence of individual sin? Do many people believe in this kind of immanent justice today?

Lk 5:27–32. The call of Levi (Mk 2:13–17 and Mt 9:9–13)

Just as Jesus claimed to be able to forgive the sins of the paralytic so here he forgives Levi's sins and Levi is enabled to embrace the kingdom of Christ. In the respectable society of the time, publicans were regarded as both traitors and excommunicates and were shunned in all decent company. Jesus' answer to the objection of the pharisees and the scribes, 5:30, brings out the central theme in Christ's teaching, that it is only the poor of heart who are able to enter into the kingdom of heaven. The publican is in a position to recognise his own need of the kingdom. For this reason he is able to accept the challenge of Christ's call and to eat and to drink with him. The scrupulously religious people, on the other hand, have numbed their sense of need of the kingdom and Jesus ironically calls them 'righteous'.

Luke follows Mark fairly closely in his account of this incident but omits that Levi was the 'son of Alphaeus'. In Mark's account Jesus seems to have had the use of a house where he was able to entertain Levi to a celebration meal. Luke changes this and makes Levi the host at Levi's house and thus avoids giving an impression which might seem to conflict with Luke's emphasis upon the homeless poverty of Jesus. The words 'to repentance' in 5:31 are found only in Luke.

How far does Jesus' attitude towards eating with tax collectors and sinners come into direct conflict with traditional teaching about avoiding bad company?

Lk 5:33–39. A question of fasting (Mk 2:18–22 and Mt 9:14–17)

This passage is included in all the three gospels in order to justify the practice of fasting in the early church. The Jewish law only required fasting on the day of atonement; the pharisees fasted twice a week on Mondays and Thursdays. The coming of the kingdom in the person of Jesus is frequently represented in the new testament as a wedding feast. Guests at a wedding would be celebrating the marriage for around one week and no fasting would be undertaken in this time; the opportunity for fasting will be after the bridegroom has died.

Verses 37–39 are a commentary on the discussion on fasting in which Jesus maintains the fundamental incompatibility of trying to link too closely the traditional religious patterns with the kind of behaviour which is appropriate now that the kingdom has dawned. The disciples of John, still apparently active even after John's arrest, were waiting for the kingdom; the coming of the bridegroom. Fasting was in their case an appropriate activity. The disciples of Jesus, however, are like the bridegroom's friends at the wedding and their role is a joyful one. The words 'then they will fast in those days' (v. 35) have been taken to mean that christians should fast during the period between the ascension of Jesus and his second coming. In their original context the words can be taken as a prophecy of future sorrow for the disciples when the crucifixion has taken place.

5:39 seems to be a tolerant observation on the part of Jesus about the impossibility of everyone being able to adapt to the new ways.

Does fasting still perform a useful religious function today? What?

Lk 6:1–11. Conflict over the sabbath (Mk 2:23–3:6 and Mt 12:1–14)

Reaping was forbidden on the sabbath and according to a legalistic understanding of this teaching Jesus' disciples were regarded as infringing the law. Reference to David is not just an appeal to precedent. Jesus is also seeking to assert that his authority is equal to that of David and that he is, in fact, the Davidic messiah. The healing of the man in the synagogue on the sabbath day makes a similar point. Jesus goes behind the legalistic interpretation of the law and points to the basic motivation behind the law. The whole Jewish law was geared to doing good; if it is doing good to heal on the sabbath day why should anybody seek to oppose it? It is interesting to note the way in which Luke deals with this Marcan passage. Mark says that Jesus was saddened and angry, Luke plays down both these elements, he also reduces the force of Mark's assertion (Mk 3:6) that the pharisees immediately went in league with the Herodians.

What are the issues to-day on which religious people might come in conflict with Jesus about the true meaning of the commandments?

Lk 6:12–16. The choice of the twelve (Mk 3:13–9 and Mt 10:1–4)

Twelve is a highly symbolic number; just as there were twelve tribes of Israel, so there were twelve people chosen by Christ to proclaim to Israel the coming of the kingdom. Luke uses the word 'apostle' six times in the gospel and eight times in the Acts. Mark and Matthew use the term only once each. The word means literally 'one who is sent' and some scholars have related it to the Jewish

concept associated with the idea of the *shaliach*: a sort
of ambassador plenipotentiary with full legal authority
to represent an important master.

Lk 6:17–27. Morality for the kingdom (Mt 5:3–12)

This is Luke's version of the sermon on the mount, although here it seems to be more like 'the sermon on the
plain'. A comparison between Luke's 'sermon on the
plain' and Matthew's 'sermon on the mount' will show
that Luke has left out a large section of teaching which
was less relevant for the gentile reader (see Mt 5 : 17–
6 : 18). Luke's sermon is also much shorter than Matthew's,
although some of the verses Luke omits appear elsewhere
in his gospel. The sermon consists first of Luke's version
of the beatitudes, verses 3–12. The poor, the hungry, the
grief-stricken and the persecuted should rejoice because
they are about to receive the kingdom of God. The rich
and the satisfied, as well as those whom the world speaks
well of, are in a quite different situation. Jesus is not
cursing them: he is asserting the reality of the situation
they have brought upon themselves.

*1. Does the church today seek to avoid being spoken
well of; would it be reasonable for it to do so?*

*2. Do you think that the church has 'pulled its punches'
when interpreting Jesus' denunciation of the rich?*

Lk 6:27–35. Indiscriminate love. (Mt 5:38–48)

This section emphasises the unconditional character of
kingdom morality. Just as God is indiscriminate (verse
35) those who accept the kingdom are invited to love all
men indiscriminately, even their enemies. Gifts and
loans and the forgiving of wrongs done are all to be

unconditional, just as God's invitation to the kingdom is unconditional. Openness to the kingdom involves a corresponding openness to others (6:36–38).

Lk 6:37–49. Sayings on charity (Mt 7:1–5 and 15–27)

These verses provide us with five assorted sayings of Christ, each bringing out fresh aspects of Jesus' moral teaching. Verse 46 shows the fatuity of a religion that is based upon words and not upon real life commitment and in verses 47–49 Jesus asserts that his moral teaching is an indispensable basis for the true following of himself.

1. Taken seriously, do you agree that Jesus' moral teaching would undermine the economy of modern western society?

2. Would those who followed Jesus' moral teaching not find that they were very vulnerable to being taken advantage of by others?

3. Does verse 27 preclude christians from taking up arms?

Lk 7:1–10. The healing of the centurion's servant (Mt 8:5–13)

As with other examples of the healing of gentiles, this miracle takes place from a distance. Jesus has come primarily to Israel. Combination of the centurion's sympathy for judaism and his awareness of himself as an outsider prevented him from presuming that he had any claim upon Jesus. Unable to put his trust in his own religion or nationality, he was able to grasp what Jesus had to offer and his servant was cured. Only Luke mentions that the centurion 'sent to him elders of the Jews', perhaps to emphasise the gulf between Jesus and this gentile.

Lk 7:11–17. The raising of the widow's son at Nain

Jesus' miracles of healing now reached their climax in the raising of a dead man to life. The early church would have interpreted this in terms of their experience of baptism; that in baptism Jesus had raised every christian from the dead. Jewish expectation of the kingdom included not only the idea of human sufferings being put to rights, but also the raising of the dead as an integral part of the reign of God upon earth. This episode is found only in Luke and it is very similar to the raising of the widow's son in 2 Kgs 4:8–37. The sites of the two miracles are remarkably close.

Lk 7:18–35. The question of John the Baptist (Mt 11:2–19)

Again, the evangelist emphasises the mission of John in relation to the ministry of Jesus. John wants to know if Jesus is genuinely the messiah. Jesus replies by alluding to Is 26:19; 29:18; 35:5–6 and 61:1. The healing of the blind and the lame, the lepers, the deaf, the raising of the dead and the proclamation of the good news to the poor are all signs of the kingdom of God. When John hears this account of the messengers it is suggested that he will understand that the kingdom has come in the person of Jesus and that Jesus is therefore the messiah. Jesus then goes on to praise the mission of John but to assert the importance of the kingdom by saying that the least in the kingdom of God is greater than John (verse 28). The point of Jesus' parable of the children in 7:31–35 is that the scribes and pharisees, the men of this generation, are like children in the market place who refuse to play at either weddings or funerals; they have taken no notice of the sombre message of John (funerals) and they have likewise ignored Jesus' joyful message of the good news (weddings).

What attitudes people have towards christians today are in any way similar to the attitudes of Jesus' contemporaries to John the Baptist and the Son of Man? (see 7 : 33–35).

Lk 7:36–50. The woman who was a sinner

To understand these verses it is necessary to realise that the woman was probably a person of promiscuous sexual habits and would therefore have been regarded as a complete outsider in respectable religious circles, then as now. We have no warrant for identifying this woman with Mary Magdalen or with Mary the sister of Martha of Bethany, and the incident seems to be quite distinct from the episodes recorded in Mk 14:3–9 and Mt 26 : 6–13. The woman in those stories is not necessarily a particularly sinful person at all. Jesus justifies his graciousness towards the woman by using the parable of two debtors, one who owes 500 denarii and the other 50. Just as the greater debtor will have stronger reason for gratitude when his debt is cancelled, so the sinner will have stronger reason for gratitude than the upright or religious person. Indeed this is just one example of an oft-repeated theme in Luke's gospel that it is those who are aware of having least claim on the kingdom who are most able to receive it.

1. Does this episode have any relevance in considering sexual permissiveness today?

2. Do christians today give too much importance to questions of sexual morality? If they do, can you suggest any reasons for this?

Lk 8:1–3. The women disciples of Jesus

In the first three verses of this chapter, Luke introduces the names of a group of women disciples of Jesus; the same women who are to be witnesses at the resurrection. These verses are peculiar to Luke and are quite typical of Luke's special emphasis on the role of women. It is important to recollect that women were not considered to be very important in contemporary society.

Do you consider that the place of women in the church today needs to be radically altered? Give reasons.

Lk 8:4–15. The parable of the sower (Mk 4:1–20 and Mt 13:1–23)

With the exception of a few words Luke's account of this parable is substantially the same as the account in Mark. When it was originally formulated the parable of the sower was probably meant to convey the teaching that the kingdom, like the harvest, had come, all appearances to the contrary notwithstanding. Just as the harvest was come even though some of the seed had not been implanted in the ground, so the kingdom had really come even though it was not universally recognised. Many scholars have suggested that verses 11–15 reflect a later interpretation of the parable where it is applied to the way in which the individual convert receives the message of the gospel and is faithful, or otherwise, to his baptismal promises.

If verses 11–15 were added later, do they not perhaps represent the beginnings of the kind of individualism which has so corrupted christian teaching through the centuries?

Lk 8:16–18. The parable of the lamp (Mk 4:21–25)
By inserting these verses at this point after the explanation of the parable of the sower, Luke wishes to apply
them to the disciples. They have understood the parable
of the sower, they are the ones who are to proclaim it.
People who have the greatest knowledge of God's kingdom have the greatest obligation to broadcast this knowledge to others.

*Can these verses be reconciled with Jesus' teaching in
Mt 6 : 1–5?*

**Lk 8:19–21. The mother and the brothers of Jesus
(Mk 3:31–35 and 12:46–50)**
These verses make a related point, the true blood relations of Jesus are those who 'hear the word of God and
do it'. In Mark the mother and brothers of Jesus in this
incident are requesting access. Perhaps out of motives of
respect Luke suggests a physical barrier, that they couldn't
reach him 'for the crowd'. In Mark Jesus seems to be
deliberately ignoring them.

*What relevance, if any, do verses 19–21 have for the
question of Mary's place in the church?*

**Lk 8:22–25. The calming of the storm (Mk 4:35–41
and Mt 8:18, 22–27)**
The Jews were a nation of land-lubbers and were profoundly afraid of the sea. The sea is often taken in the
bible as a metaphor for evil and chaos. At creation God
brings order out of a watery chaos (Gen 1 : 2) and in the
vision of God's final victory in Revelation it says that
there will be no more sea (Rev 21 : 1). By rebuking the

winds and the waves and establishing his authority over the sea, Jesus identifies with Yahweh in the first act of creation and demonstrates the power of the messiah over all principles of evil chaos.

How far are nature miracles of this kind credible for twentieth-century man?

Lk 8:26–39. The Gerasene demoniac (Mk 5:1–20 and Mt 8:28–34)

This story conveys substantially the same lesson as the stilling of the waves. Jesus goes out into a Gentile region and there, among the tombs, places of ritual defilement, Jesus encounters a particularly bad case of demoniac possession. Once more his messianic power is vindicated and the man is healed. Only Luke adds the flourish that the demons were thrown 'into the abyss', the place where they properly belonged.

Lk 8:40–56. The healing of Jairus' daughter, and the woman with the flow of blood (Mk 5:21–43 and Mt 9:18–26)

Jesus is on his way to cure the daughter of Jairus, a synagogue official, when a haemophiliac woman touched the border of his garment. If, as has been suggested, the woman was suffering from a menstrual disorder, this would have rendered her ritually unclean and unable to take part in any official religious practices. Although her approach to Jesus is rather superstitious, by modern standards, the underlying faith is sufficient for her to be healed. The raising of Jairus' daughter makes the same point as the raising of the widow's son in 7:11–17. Jesus not only heals particular disorders, he completely changes the whole human condition, raising mortal man to a new level of existence.

Is it possible, as with the woman with the flow of blood, that superstition may sometimes serve as a mask for a very real faith?

Lk 9:1–6. The mission of the twelve (Mk 6:7–16 and Mt 10:5, 8–14 and 14:1)

The twelve apostles are sent out to preach the good news of the kingdom to the twelve tribes of Israel. The number twelve signifies that Jesus is calling a new Israel and they are invited not to put their trust in any provisions that they are able to make for their mission.

Is the church as an institution justified in investing its money today? Should individual christians have investments?

Omitting Mark's longer account of the execution (Mk 6:17–29) Luke chooses this point to refer to John's execution by Herod.

Lk 9:10–17. The feeding of the five thousand (Mk 6:30–44; Mt 14:13–21 and Jn 6:1–13)

This feeding miracle refers back to the feeding of Israel in the wilderness and it also foreshadows the feeding of the church in the eucharist. The number five thousand represents the perfection of all Israel. Like Israel in the exodus from Egypt, the people are in a desert place. The twelve baskets which are picked up afterwards relate to the twelve tribes of Israel. The two fishes are a possible reference to Num 11:22 and 32 where Israel in the

desert was fed with food from the sea. Jesus then, like his
Father, feeds the people of God in the desert. In 9:16
'He looked up to heaven and blessed and broke them and
gave them' there is a fourfold action reminiscent of some
of the earliest texts for the eucharist. The fact that there
are twelve baskets left over suggests that Jesus not only
satisfied the people's hunger; he more than satisfied it.

Lk 9:18–22. Peter's profession of faith and the first prophecy of the passion (Mk 8:27–32 and Mt 16:13–21)

Here Peter identifies Jesus as the messiah and Jesus replies by asserting that the messiah is not only the Son of
Man, he is also the suffering servant of Is 53, the innocent
victim whose sufferings would reconcile Israel to God.

Lk 9:23–27. Carrying of the cross (Mk 8:34–9:1 and Mt 16:24–27)

The service of the messiah and of his kingdom then involves sharing in the role of the suffering servant. The
service of the kingdom involves the type of commitment
in which one is prepared to lose everything, even life
itself. Verse 25 could be translated: 'what does it profit
a man if he gains the whole world and ceases to be a real
person?' Jesus does not clearly identify himself as the
'Son of Man' here, although the identification is no doubt
intended by Luke.

   *The 'penny' catechism quoted verse 25 in answer to the
question 'of which must you take most care, of your body
or of your soul?' Is this just a harmless mistranslation or
has it contributed towards a neurotic attitude toward the
body and an alienated attitude towards involvement in
the secular sphere?*

Lk 9:27. The coming kingdom (Mk 9:1 and Mt 16:28)

This verse has been taken to refer to the destruction of Jerusalem, to the resurrection and ascension of Christ, which are foreshadowed in the episode of the transfiguration which follows immediately, and they have been used in order to demonstrate that either Jesus or the evangelists held a genuinely mistaken view about the proximity of the second coming.

Lk 9:28–36. The transfiguration (Mk 9:2–8 and Mt 17:1–8)

As with the temptation in the desert and the feeding of the five thousand, we are again reminded of the exodus (Ex 24:16–18). Like Moses, Jesus goes up into a mountain and is transfigured and hears a voice speaking out of the cloud. Moses represents the law and Elijah represents the prophets. Both the law and the prophets are fulfilled in Christ. The point about 'the eighth day' is that the first day of the week was the day of the resurrection; the world was considered to have been made in seven days. The eighth day, the first day of the new week, was the day of the new creation in Christ. Either the transfiguration foreshadowed the resurrection, or else, as some scholars suggest, it is really an account of a post-resurrection episode which the synoptic writers have placed earlier in the text. At all events the transfiguration is very closely linked with the resurrection. Peter's request in verse 33 has to be understood in the light of the prophecy in Zechariah 14:16 where the imagery of the feast of tents is applied to the future kingdom. The feast of tents, originally a harvest festival, served to remind the Jews of the time when they lived in tents in the desert.

Zechariah foresees a golden future when the gentiles will all come to Jerusalem to join in the feast of tents. Peter's suggestion 'to make three booths' is really affirming that this messianic age has now come, in the person of the glorified Christ. But he has failed to understand Jesus' identification of himself as the suffering servant. The kingdom has come but suffering and struggle are still necessary.

How far is the church genuinely international?

Lk 9:37–43. The epileptic (Mk 9:14–27 and Mt 17:14–18)

Just as Moses experienced disillusion on coming down from the glory of Mount Sinai, so Jesus experiences disillusion on coming down from Mount Transfiguration. With Moses the disillusion was the result of the Israelites worshipping the golden calf. With Jesus it is the result of the disciples being unable to heal through lack of faith.

Would more miracles of healing take place today if christians had more faith?

Lk 9:44–50. The second prediction of the passion (Mk 9:30–50 and Mt 17:22–18:35)

Once more Jesus is reported as identifying his role not only as messiah, Son of Man, but also as the suffering servant. The failure of the disciples to understand this identification is underlined by their quarrel over which of them has the most exalted status. Jesus' response indicates the quality of childhood which the true servants of the suffering messiah must strive to cultivate. Like children they must rely on their Father's love rather than upon their own merits, real or imagined. Typical of the disciples' self-importance in the service of the kingdom is their rebuke of the strange exorcist in verse 49. Jesus' reply urges them to see such persons as allies rather than rivals.

1. To what extent is it true that 9 : 48 and its parallels in Matthew and Mark have been misrepresented as an exhortation to religious infantilism?

2. Does 9 : 50 have any relevance to the ecumenical movement?

3. Some scholars claim to discern in the words in 9 : 47–48 some technical terms relating to baptism, and use these verses as support for the practice of infant baptism. What are the advantages and disadvantages of this practice?

4

The journey to Jerusalem
Lk 9:51–19:27

From 9:51 to 18:14 has been called the 'long interpolation' as it represents a major break in the framework taken over from Mark, and includes many episodes which are only found in Luke. The placing of all the events and sayings in this section in the context of a journey from Galilee to Jerusalem is clearly a very artificial arrangement. Luke is extremely vague about the exact geographical location of many of the events he records and it is clear that his main interest is in giving dramatic emphasis to Jerusalem: the centre where the Lord is to be crucified and from which the good news of the resurrection will go out. In the same way Luke suppresses all mention of any resurrection appearances in Galilee at the end of his gospel.

Lk 9:51–60. The Samaritan village

This is the only episode in any of the gospels where Jesus encounters hostility from the Samaritans. Just as the section on the Galilean ministry of Jesus (4:14–9:50) began with the rejection of Jesus at his native village of Nazareth so this section begins with the rejection of Jesus by a Samaritan village. The theme of rejection in both cases sets the mood for the final climax of his death in

Jerusalem. The Samaritan villagers were probably indulging in religious prejudice against Jews going to Jerusalem rather than to the rival Samaritan shrine at Mount Gerizim. Jesus refuses to respond to religious hatred in kind or to go along with the patriotic fanaticism of James and John. The mention of fire being 'called down from heaven to consume them' is an echo of 2 Kgs 1 where Elijah is represented as calling down fire from heaven upon the messengers of the King of Samaria. Jesus is different from Elijah in this sense.

Should the church ever accept military protection, for example, against atheistic communism?

Lk 9:57–62. Commitment to the apostolate (Mt 8:19–22)

Luke here records Jesus' response to three would-be preachers of the kingdom. The first is reminded that Jesus and his disciples live the unsettled lives of vagrants. The second and third plead family loyalty and duty. In each case Jesus' reply underlines the all-or-nothing character of serving the kingdom. The situation is too urgent to allow of delay. The man in verses 61 and 62 reminds us again of Elijah (1 Kgs 19:19–21) Elijah calls Elisha while he is working at the plough, and allows him to 'say farewell to those at home'. Again Jesus is different from Elijah. The mission of preaching the kingdom is too pressing to admit of even this much delay.

1. Have christians lost the sense of the urgency of their mission? If so, why?
2. Would the gospel have more impact if christians lived in less comfort?

Lk 10:1–12. The mission of the seventy-two

The theme of the urgency of the disciples' task in preaching the kingdom is carried over into this section. Matthew and Mark record the detailed instructions in connection with the twelve. Luke is alone in referring to a mission of the seventy-two (in some manuscripts, seventy). The 'harvest' is the kingdom and the urgency of the disciples' task makes it necessary for them to pray for more helpers (10:2). They are warned to go unencumbered with unnecessary luggage (10:4) and not to waste time chattering with passers-by. They are to accept hospitality (10:7) and to publicly proclaim the imminence of the kingdom (10:10). Refusal to accept the message will bring its own retribution (10:10–16).

In what ways might these verses be usefully adopted by clergy or missionaries today? Which injunctions, if any, are no longer practicable?

Lk 10:13–16. The consequences of rejecting the kingdom (Mt 11:20–24 and 10:40)

The first two verses here provide us with Jesus' lament over Chorazin, Bethsaida and Capernaum. In Matthew these verses are provoked by the lack of faith of the citizens of these three Galilean towns, even after Jesus had performed miracles among them. In their Lucan context these verses make less sense, since the mission of the seventy-two appears to have been a success. Comparatively recent (1905 and 1926) excavations in a basalt desert some two miles north west of Capernaum have uncovered quite a substantial town with its own synagogue which is believed to be Chorazin.

Lk 10:17–24. The return of the seventy-two

The seventy return with triumph from their mission of preaching the kingdom and report the successful casting out of the demons in the name of Jesus. Jesus' reply, 'I saw Satan fall like lightning from heaven' has often been applied to the traditional fall of Lucifer before the creation of the world. This belief originated with the church father Origen in the third century and was applied both to this passage and to the account of the 'war in heaven' in Rev 12. The real meaning of Jesus' words, based perhaps on Is 14:12, is probably that in the preaching of the kingdom by the seventy-two, not only have demons been cast out, but Satan himself has been deprived of his power. Their real cause for rejoicing, however, should not be that they have had power over evil spirits but that they have been chosen and that their names are written in the book of life (10:20). Jesus then thanks his Father for the role that they have been allowed to play; nobody can understand the true relationship between the Father and the Son except those whom the Father has chosen (10:22). The religious men and the theologians, 'the wise and understanding', have not understood this relationship between the Father and the Son. On the contrary, this knowledge has been given to the babes, mere children with no real knowledge of the law (10:21). In these verses Jesus claims such a unique relationship with the Father that some critics have refused to believe that these verses are genuine to Luke, on the grounds that they seem to reflect a later theology of the incarnation. There is, however, no solid basis for this scepticism. In 10:24 Jesus asserts that in his own person he has fulfilled the whole of old testament history. Many 'prophets and kings' had longed for the kingdom of God's messiah, now it had come; the disciples had experienced it directly. Verses 21–24 are also found in Mt 11:25–27.

1. If christianity can be accepted by anyone with simple faith is there any necessity for a sophisticated theology?

2. Do you think that the church should still resort to exorcisms today? In particular would they have any place in missionary work where dealing with people who believed in the power of evil spirits in much the same way as did the people of new testament times?

Lk 10:25–37. The law of love and the parable of the good Samaritan

Quoting Deuteronomy 6:5 and Leviticus 19:18, Jesus summarizes the entire Jewish law under the headings of 'love of God' and 'love of neighbour'. It does not necessarily suggest a 'situation ethic' to say that love is the only moral absolute. It was after all St Augustine who said 'Love and do what you like'. The lawyer, one with special knowledge of the *torah,* is dissatisfied with Jesus' reply. Loving, after all, is a very open-ended type of commitment; how could he be sure that he was being righteous (10:29)? In order to determine this he asks who is to be regarded as his neighbour. The parable of the good Samaritan does not quite answer the question; instead Jesus leaves the lawyer with the question of who 'proved neighbour to the man who fell among robbers'? The answer in this case is not the priest or the levite, religious men scrupulously following the law, but an outsider of polluted stock and with heretical religious beliefs. Love of neighbour, then, is a principle which transcends all ethnic or religious considerations. There is no-one that followers of Jesus are not able to call neighbour.

1. Discuss a possible twentieth-century parallel to this parable which makes the same fundamental points.

2. Can a sound morality be based solely or even primarily upon desire for heavenly reward? or on love?

Lk 10:38–42. Martha and Mary

These verses have often been used by Roman catholic spiritual writers to show the greater value of contemplative over active life. This is not, of course, their original meaning. The fundamental point that is being made here is that Jesus' teaching on the kingdom has an absolute priority over every other consideration.

It would be rather too easy to jump to the conclusion that the village referred to in verse 38 was Bethany, the home of Martha, Mary and Lazarus as referred to in Jn 11:1, but it does seem at least possible that Luke and John have both drawn from the same material at this point. If this were the case, however, 'it might seem strange that Luke should omit so striking a story as the raising of Lazarus' (Leaney).

Do purely contemplative religious orders in fact fulfil any real purpose in the modern world?

Lk 11:1–4. The Lord's prayer (Mt 6:9–13)

Only Luke introduces this section with Jesus at prayer: a typically Lucan touch. It is interesting to compare this version of the Lord's prayer with that found in Matthew (6:9–13). Luke's version is shorter and may well be the earlier version. The word 'Father' here is the equivalent of the Aramaic *Abba* and is an intimate term usually used within the family circle and not previously applied to

God within the tradition of judaism. The unique sonship which Jesus claimed for himself in 10:21 is to be shared with all those who follow Christ. The petition 'hallowed be thy name' is a request for God to reveal his glory. 'Thy kingdom come' is the main point of the prayer. God can be addressed as a familiar father; he will manifest his glory through the coming of his kingdom. The kingdom is already present in the person of Christ but it is still necessary to pray for its final manifestation. 'Thy will be done on earth as it is in heaven' tells us something of the character of God's kingdom; when God's kingdom has fully come on earth, it will be acknowledged by everybody and his will will be manifest in everything. 'Give us each day our daily bread' is a prayer for the daily necessities of life and as understood in the early church might conceivably have included the bread of the eucharist. Matthew's 'give us today our bread of tomorrow' may in this case be the more primitive version making the petition a prayer for a sharing in the final banquet of the kingdom. 'Forgive us our sins for we ourselves forgive everyone who is indebted to us' reminds us of the parable of the two debtors in Matthew 18. In the face of the coming kingdom we are all obliged to forgive debts as freely as we ask our own debts to be forgiven. God will accept us unconditionally and we in turn must have an unconditional openness towards others. The last petition too is offered in view of the imminent coming of God's kingdom and might be translated 'do not allow us to be defeated when the final test comes'.

1. Is it appropriate that most christian prayer should be offered to God the Father?

2. Is Jesus providing his disciples with a structure to their prayer or is he giving them a formula for their repetition? Do you think the 'our Father' could be used profitably as either?

3. Do we or can we mean it when we pray for the final coming of the kingdom?

Lk 11:5–13. Teaching on prayer

These verses really form a commentary on the Lord's prayer which has preceded them. The first parable of the friend at midnight refers to the earlier part of the prayer: when we pray for the coming of God's kingdom we must be persistent like the neighbour who keeps on pestering until he receives the favour he demands. The second set of sayings emphasise God's readiness to grant the petitions of the Lord's prayer. If sinful human beings are ready to satisfy their children's real needs, then, Jesus argues, how much more will the Father give the Holy Spirit, the active principle of God's activity in the last days (Acts 2). Verses 9–13 are paralleled in Mt 7:7–11.

Does prayer really change anything, if so, what? Does it change our own attitudes, God's mercy, or the course of natural events?

Lk 11:14–26. Teaching on evil spirits (Mt 12:22–30; also Mt 9:32–34 and Mk 3:22–30)

Jesus demonstrates that he is not exorcizing through the power of Beelzebul, the prince of devils, on the grounds that, if he were, Beelzebul would be undermining his own kingdom: the kingdom which is, even now, giving way to the kingdom of God (11:20). The parable of the unclean spirit in verses 24 to 26 is a commentary on verse 23. The power of evil has indeed been smashed by the coming of God's kingdom in Christ, but it is not possible to be neutral in the struggle. Anyone who attempts to stand on the sidelines will be worse off than if the kingdom had never in fact come.

The exact identity of Beelzebul is not clear and the name contains echoes of more than one demonology. The 'your sons' of verse 19 is a reference to other contemporary exorcists. They were just as vulnerable as Jesus to this kind of slander. The reference to 'the finger of God' is not as crude as it sounds but serves to underline that Jesus is the second Moses. In Ex 8 : 19 the magicians of Pharaoh have to concede 'This is the finger of God'. Some Jewish commentators made it clear that when Pharaoh's magicians did perform their magic they did so by the agency of demons.

Satan is the 'strong man fully armed' of verse 21 and Jesus is the 'one stronger than he' who conquers and seizes his adversary's armour as a trophy.

1. Is 11 : 23 a flat contradiction of the saying in 9 : 50?
2. Given all the complexities involved in believing or, indeed, just living, is it possible to be wholly committed? Could it not be argued that commitment to the gospel is an unbalanced response in the face of the ambiguity of the evidence?

Lk 11:27–28. The blessedness of Mary

The woman's acclamation in verse 27 is intended as a compliment both to Jesus and to his mother. Jesus makes the same point here as in 8 : 19–21. True blessedness does not consist in blood kinship with Jesus, but in commitment to his teaching. In the catholic tradition 11 : 28 has been taken to mean that Mary is not blessed primarily as the physical mother of Jesus, but as the model of obedience to the word of God. (cf 1 : 38).

Can you explain the existence of the more unbalanced sort of devotion to Mary which is sometimes observable? Have many catholics gone too far the other way since Vatican II?

Lk 11:29–32. The sign of Jonah (Mt 12:39–42)

Here Jesus claims that the crowds were seeking for a definitive sign that he was the messiah and that the kingdom had come. The only sign that would be given to them would be the sign of the resurrection: 'the sign of Jonah' who was three days in the belly of a whale. The 'queen of the South' (1 Kgs 10) and the repentent Ninevites (Jon 3:4–10) both stand in judgement on Jesus' contemporaries, as Jesus is of far greater significance than either Solomon or Jonah.

Ought christians to try to produce convincing arguments for the resurrection from the historical evidence available? Would these arguments contribute to spreading real faith?

Lk 11:33–36. Sayings on light (Mt 5:15; 6:22f, and Mk 4:21)

The *torah*, or law, was often spoken of as a lamp. The light referred to in verse 33 might conceivably be Jesus or it might be the witness of believers. If it is a reference to Jesus then it continues the theme of 11:29–32, that Jesus himself is a sign to the evil generation. This verse is more commonly supposed to refer to the necessity of a bold witness to the kingdom. Having received the light of Christ we have an obligation to extend his light to the whole world (11:34–36). 11:33 is partly a repetition of Lk 8:16.

Is church life too inward looking? Is this a failure of individuals or structures?

Lk 11:37–54. Woes against the pharisees and lawyers (Mt 23:1–36)

These verses consist of a savage denunciation of the religious people of Christ's day. Pharisees believed in 'building a hedge around the *torah*': supplementing the written law of Moses contained in the Pentateuch with an unwritten law consisting chiefly of a host of detailed instructions. Jesus denounces this scrupulous religiosity which so frequently overlooks the real fundamentals. The doctors of the law too (11:45) come under the same condemnation. Multiplication of religious practices all too easily led people to a false estimate of themselves; only those who knew their poverty before God were able to accept his kingdom.

In the light of the ferocity of these verses are we to detect a moral weakness in Jesus, or have we given too much importance to notions of gentleness and tolerance in our idea of love of neighbour?

Lk 12:1–12. Witnessing to Christ (Mt 10:26–33; 12:32 and 10:19f)

The disciples are here exhorted to be as unlike the pharisees as possible. The pharisees in their false estimate of themselves were hypocrites and were afraid of the truth. With the coming of the kingdom their secret inner corruption, present like leaven in the dough, would be clearly visible (1–3). The followers of Jesus by contrast are to give bold testimony to the truth even when this involves the possibility of martyrdom (12:4–12).

Do you agree that it is reasonable to suppose that christians would endure a great deal more persecution today if they were not hypocrites?

Lk 12:13–34. Teaching on riches

The rich fool in the parable (12:13–21) is almost a classic case of inauthentic existence and is offered in response to the question of the man in verse 13. All should be warned by the total preoccupation of one fool with greater material prosperity and security. The fact of death shows the hollowness of these false priorities. Only in this parable and perhaps in the other parable of a rich man in Luke 16 is individual death seen as bringing crisis and judgement. In every other case it is the imminent public manifestation of the kingdom which performs this function. The effect, however, is the same; to be preoccupied with things which have no lasting value is stupid.

12:22–34 (cf Mt 6:25–33) further elaborate this theme. Unlike the rich fool, the disciples are to be quite unconcerned about material security. The seeking of the kingdom must be their total preoccupation (12:31). Verse 32 reiterates that the kingdom is the gift of God. Material status all too easily gives people illusions about themselves. Only those who are able to let go of everything are in a position to accept the kingdom as pure gift. The little flock (12:32) can practice personal poverty in the knowledge that the kingdom is the Father's gift. Their treasure is completely secure (33–34).

1. How far do you find these teachings in conflict with middle-class values?

2. Is it possible for a christian to be rich and at the same time remain faithful to his calling?

3. Is it possible to live in a capitalist society without being spiritually impoverished?

Lk 12:35–58. Readiness for the kingdom (Mt 24: 43–51)

These verses relate to the kingdom as something still in the future. The disciples are to be like servants who do not know exactly when their master will return (12:35–38). The Son of Man will come unexpectedly like a burglar (12:39–40 cf Mt 24:43 f). Constant vigilance is the only answer. The parable of the servant waiting for his master's return (cf Mt 24:45–51) is very like 12:35–38, although in this case there is only one servant involved and he has been placed in a position of considerable trust. Jesus spells out several possible courses of action for the servant together with their consequences (12:41–48; cf Mt 24:45–51). Originally all the parables and sayings in this passage may have been directed at the leaders of the Jewish religion of the time. The kingdom would be upon them when they least anticipated it and they would be compelled to give an account of their stewardship. Like Matthew in his parallel sections (24:43–25:30), Luke has re-applied these verses to the situation of the church waiting for the second coming of Christ. The burning lamps and the master returning home from a marriage are very reminiscent of the parable of the wise and foolish virgins in Mt 25:1–13.

Have christians ceased to live in the expectation of the second coming of Christ? If so, can you suggest reasons? Has any important perspective been lost in the process?

Lk 12:49–53. The necessity for decision (Mt 10:34–36)

There is nothing 'meek and mild' about the Jesus of these
verses. The image of 'fire' (12 : 49) still has power to con-
jure up images of judgement, revolution and destructive
violence. Jesus himself will be obliged to suffer the 'baptism' of a violent death (12 : 50). He is not immediately
bringing in a reign of peace but a principle of disruption
into human relationships. There can be no neutrality
about the kingdom and a right decision may easily involve conflict with those with whom one has the strongest
natural ties (a fulfilment of the prophecy in Mic 7 : 6).

*What do you think of the argument that the gospel
has been 'tamed' and has been used as a prop for the
'status quo'? If so, who has tamed it and why? Is religion
of necessity 'the opium of the people'?*

Lk 12:54–13:9. The coming crisis (Mt 16:2f and 5:25f)

In these verses Jesus draws attention to the unambiguous
character of his teaching and mission. How can his hearers recognise changes in the weather and not recognise
that the kingdom is imminent (12 : 54–56)? They are in
the critical situation of being defendants in the dock (12 :
57–59). He rejects the idea that individual misfortune
represents punishment for individual sin (13 : 1–4) but
urges repentance as the only possible preparation for the
universal judgement of the coming kingdom (13 : 5)
Luke's parable of the fig tree (13 : 6–9) replaces the cursing of the barren fig tree in Mark and Matthew. In both
cases the fig tree is a symbol of Israel (see Jer 8 : 13 and
Hos 9 : 10). If Israel does not repent then she will be
rejected.

Do these verses imply that there is a limit to God's patience? If they do, does this mean that there is a limit to his love? Does it help to resolve this difficulty by simply saying that Jesus is using language of crisis?

Lk 13:10–17. A sabbath healing

Only Luke records this parable and it is quite characteristic of Luke in its emphasis both on Jesus' concern for pathetic cases and on the full availability of the kingdom to women as much as to men. It should be remembered that women enjoyed only an inferior status in the synagogue congregation. Some contemporary commentaries on sabbath observance stipulated that it was an offence to untie knots on the sabbath day. Technically Jesus was infringing this particular piece of legalism and he provokes a direct confrontation with the equivalent of the presiding minister. Here as elsewhere Jesus appeals to the true spirit of the law in order to refute religious sophistry, and as far as the ordinary people are concerned it is Jesus who gets the best of the argument.

Is there a christian dimension to the struggle for women's rights?

Lk 13:18–21. Two parables of the kingdom (Mt 13:31–33; Mk 4:30–32)

The inclusion of these two parables at this point may be intended to emphasise the way the developing power of the kingdom has suddenly begun to have its full impact for people like the deformed woman in the previous verses. Both parables make clear that the kingdom is a pure gift of God. The gradual development of the seed into a tree or the rising of the leavening dough are not

observable to the human eye but they are real nonethe-
less. It must have been hard for Jesus' contemporaries to
believe that one travelling preacher and his rustic companions somehow embodied the dawning of the kingdom
of God upon human history, but Jesus teaches that the
whole movement of history is irreversibly directed towards the certain coming of the kingdom. Unlike all
purely human revolutions God's revolution does not de-
pend upon human co-operation. It is a gift, and the gift
is already acting as a leaven in human history.

*Is there a danger of regarding the coming of the king-
dom with a fatalistic attitude of resignation?*

Lk 13:22–35. The narrow door (Mt 7:13f; 25:10; 7:22f; 8:11f; 23:37–39)

Because the kingdom is a gift it is difficult for men to
enter into it. Jesus refuses to give a direct answer to the
question in 13:23. His words do not attempt to deal with
the question of how many, but with the question of how
difficult. In particular, it is difficult for those with the privilege of Jewish religion and Jewish nationality to accept
the kingdom. The kingdom could only be accepted as gift
and those who felt most entitled to it would find it most
difficult to accept it. In contrast those with the least claim
upon the kingdom, the gentiles, would find themselves
participating fully in the banquet of the messiah.

At this point Jesus is warned against Herod and he replies by flinging down a ferocious taunt. In any case, he
argues, he is destined to suffer at Jerusalem, and not in
Galilee. Luke then inserts the words of Jesus' lament over
Jerusalem which Matthew places more suitably during

holy week. It is Jerusalem, the powerful symbol of institutional religion, which has the tradition of killing the prophets and its refusal to accept the kingdom will bring about its own downfall.

Do you agree that the christian church has contributed to anti-semitism by applying Jesus' judgement on Jerusalem to judaism in particular instead of upon institutional religion as a whole? Can you think of any church or sect which has not 'persecuted the prophets'?

Lk 14:1–24. Against discrimination

Luke has brought together one healing miracle and three parables in the theme of meals and represented them as all taking place during a meal at a pharisee's house. It is, of course, unlikely that the original episodes were linked in this way and the arrangement demonstrates a skilful piece of editing technique. The healing of the dropsied man (1–6) is found only in Luke but it makes the same point as the healing of the man in Lk 6:9 (Mk 3:4; Mt 12:10) and in the healing of the woman in Lk 13:10, that love represents a principle more than any human interpretation of the law of Moses and that Jesus, as the messiah, claims the authentic right to interpret afresh the meaning of the commandments.

The first of the three meal-parables (7–11) provides a warning against the natural human propensity to self-importance. The second (12–14) invites us to a completely indiscriminate openness towards others. These injunctions are not merely extremely difficult pieces of advice about the ordering of our social lives. The parable of the great supper (Luke's rather different version of Mt 22:1–10) puts both the earlier parables in their proper

context. The marriage feast is a symbol of the kingdom.
God's invitation is indiscriminate and quite gratuitous.
It is not the worthy people who are invited but those
who have least claim: 'the poor, the blind and the lame.'
If the guest-list is composed on this basis it is clear that
no one has any cause either for self-congratulation (7–11)
or for discrimination against others (12–14). These les-
sons were intended primarily as notice to the pharisees
and other scrupulously religious persons that they had
no special or exclusive claim in the kingdom, but they
also supply an impressive challenge to the whole ordering of modern society and the relationship between its
members.

*1. To what degree does the structure of our society
revolve around the varying degrees of acceptability of
our neighbours?*

*2. Do you agree that many advertisements utilise the
kind of self-assertion reproved in 14 : 7–11?*

*3. What relevance, if any, do verses 7–11 have upon
questions of immigration controls; class, colour and religious discrimination?*

*4. Do these passages have any relevance for the ecu-
menical movement, especially for the question of inter-
communion at the eucharist?*

Lk 14:25–35. The cost of discipleship (Mt 10:37f; 5:13; Mk 9:50)

Luke now moves from the theme of the ready availability
of the kingdom and includes a number of sayings in
which Jesus dwells upon the terrible and exclusive demands which service of the kingdom will involve. The
claims of the kingdom will override all considerations of

family loyalty and responsibility (14:26). In the last analysis the disciple must be prepared to follow Christ even to the gallows (14:27). Great crowds are following Jesus (14:25) and Jesus offers them two parables which invite them to reflect upon the decisive nature of a free acceptance of his kingdom (14:28–33). A half-hearted follower is like salt that has become useless for its true purpose (14:34–35).

1. These words have often been applied to vocation to the priesthood or the religious life. How far would you agree that this application of the words has contributed to the belief that it is not necessary for the ordinary church member to be fully committed?

2. Was Jesus a fanatic? Does he invite his disciples to be fanatics also? Justify your replies.

Lk 15:1–32. Three parables of forgiveness (Mt 18:12–14)

Here as elsewhere Jesus scandalises the virtuous and religious by receiving and eating with moral and religious outsiders (1–2). The mention of eating returns us to the theme of gratuitous invitations to the banquet of the messiah in chapter 14. The parable of the lost sheep, found also in Matthew, and the parable of the lost coin, which is peculiar to Luke, both make the same point. Jesus is amply justified in concentrating primarily on the complete outsider just as ordinary people are justified in giving priority to searching for their lost possessions. The parable of the prodigal son expands this theme. The elder brother is quite ungracious to resent his father's forgiveness and generosity towards the younger brother. Similarly the genuinely pious people have no cause to resent

the generosity of the Father, as revealed in the actions of
Jesus towards the tax-collectors and sinners.

*Should churches and clergy concentrate primarily on
the spiritual care of church members or upon their mission to the outsiders? Can you suggest any way of recon-
ciling the apparently conflicting demands of these two
activities?*

Lk 16:1–16. Uses and abuses of money

Apart from the largely inexplicable interruption of
verses 16–18 the entire chapter is given over to the subject of money. The parable of the unjust steward which
begins the section is perhaps the most difficult of all the
parables to understand. It is more likely that the 'master'
who commended the unjust steward in verse 9 is intended
to mean Jesus rather than the employer the steward has
swindled. In this form the parable might have been intended to serve as an example of admirable resourceful-
ness in a crisis situation. Faced with the crisis situation
of the coming kingdom, Jesus recommends that his hearers (perhaps not originally the disciples) should be equally
resourceful in the things of God. There are several other
possible interpretations. According to one view the
steward was abetting the landowner in extortion and is
only able to abandon this immoral practice when faced
with a reckoning; faced with imminent judgement Jesus'
hearers too will find an additional motivation for the
right use of money. Perhaps reflecting another interpretation offered by Luke himself, verse nine seems to draw
the very general lesson that we have to be ready to make
the very best use of the financial resources available to us.
In verses ten to twelve this meaning is turned on its head.

The lesson now drawn makes the steward an example of how *not* to behave, and the lesson to be drawn is that nobody is only a little bit dishonest. Luke continues this largely unconnected set of sayings with the famous saying, shared with Matthew, on the utter impossibility of combining service of God with service of material possessions (JB 'money'). Verses 14–15 record a conflict of opinion with the pharisees over this point. The pharisees foreshadowed the modern protestant capitalist ethic in regarding material success as a sign of God's favour and as reward for virtue. Virtue, in the teaching of Jesus, however, is not discernible in terms of economic status (16:15).

How far do we attempt to serve both God and Mammon as a church; as a nation; or as individuals? Are there any practicable alternatives?

Lk 16:16–18. Three sayings (Mt 11:12f; 5:18, 32)

There now follow three apparently unrelated sayings of Jesus. Perhaps the connection can be made as follows. The law had been normative until John and now while men enter forcefully into the kingdom the law still has value. As an example of the law being amplified rather than abrogated, Luke then instances Jesus' teaching on divorce.

1. Does Jesus' teaching on divorce still carry the same force for couples in the changed social conditions of the twentieth century?

2. Granting the moral validity of Christ's teaching on divorce, is it reasonable for christians to exert political pressure to prevent more permissive divorce laws from being enacted?

Lk 16:19–31. The rich man and Lazarus

Luke now returns to the theme of riches. Referring back
to verse 14 it seems likely that this parable was being told
against the pharisees who were 'lovers of money' and
trusted in being sons of Abraham. Jesus makes full use
of the mythology of the time. In the judaism of the period
the dead were thought to wait in Sheol for the general
resurrection. Those who were waiting peacefully would
be waiting in Abraham's 'bosom' whereas the wicked
would be waiting in a state of torment. God's verdict on
the rich man in the story is seen as totally reversing the
world's verdict. The rich man's lofty status does not help
him to find salvation any more than Lazarus' poverty pre-
vents him from finding his. The point of verse 29 is that
the message of the law and the prophets should have been
clear enough; the only other sign that the rich and religious will get is the sign of the prophet Jonah, the resurrection of Christ, and verse 31 indicates that even this
may not produce the necessary change of heart.

*It is easy to say that we, in the developed countries, are
the rich man and the poor of the third world are Lazarus;
what would repentance really involve for us as individuals, as a society, as a church?*

Lk 17:1–10. Miscellaneous sayings

Luke has here brought together a number of sayings; on
giving scandal to 'little ones' (17:1–3, cf Mt 18:6 f. and
Mk 9:42); on forgiveness (17:3–4); exhortation to a completely unconditional faith (17:5–6; cf Mt 17:20; 21:21
and Mk 11:22); and a parable exhibiting the truly open-
ended character of the service of the kingdom (17:7–10).
The kingdom of God is not given in response to human

merit. It is a completely free gift. In entering the kingdom we are quite gratuitously forgiven and we must be prepared to forgive just as freely. The gift of the kingdom is so tremendous that from then onwards we are able to believe anything. The normal bounds of possibility have already been surpassed. So too with the moral law of the kingdom. At no point are we able to say that we have kept the rules and are therefore all right with God. Because God gives us so much in giving us the kingdom our response can never be measured.

1. *Do you agree that an open-minded morality is more demanding than a legalistic one? Are the ten commandments a suitable basis for teaching christian morality?*

2. *Even allowing for the semitic hyperbole in the sayings on faith and forgiveness here, how could one answer the objection that it is unreasonable to impose no limits whatever upon both faith and forgiveness?*

Lk 17:11–19. The ten lepers

This story is only found in Luke and it is typical of Luke's gospel that this should be so. Lepers were excluded from all religious worship and were avoided by all pious Jews, not just because they were a health hazard, but also because they were ritually unclean. The kingdom which Jesus brings is inclusive of all those who were outside the scope of the Jewish law. That a Samaritan should be the only one to return to give thanks reinforces the point. This Samaritan was not only a leper, he was also, as a Samaritan, both religiously schismatic and of mixed Jewish and gentile stock.

Who are the 'lepers' of our society and how can we best help them?

Lk 17:20–37. The kingdom of God

The question posed by the pharisees presupposes that the kingdom of God is coming in the future. Jesus asserts that the kingdom of God has already arrived in his own person: 'the kingdom of God is in the midst of you.' The translation 'within you' is not very plausible and has contributed considerably to an exaggerated religious individualism. The verses which follow indicate that the final consummation of the kingdom will only come after a great deal of tribulation and catastrophe, both for Christ and for his followers. When it does come it will take everybody by surprise just as in the case of the flood in Genesis and the destruction of Sodom. Those who really seek to embrace the kingdom must be prepared to gamble everything upon it. The question the disciples ask in verse 37 seems to presuppose that the kingdom would take place at a particular geographical point. Jesus replies that the judgement will come wherever there are human beings to be judged.

In what sense can we say that judgement is already a fact now?

Lk 18:1–8. The unjust judge

The point of this parable is the same as that in the parable of the friend at midnight, Lk 11:5–8, namely that we should demand and long for the justice of God's kingdom. The point is that if even an unjust judge will give in to the relentless pestering of a widow, how much more can God's children expect their prayer and perseverance to be vindicated by the coming of the kingdom.

Are there any grounds for supposing that a crude in-

terpretation of this parable might lead to the idea of prayer of petition being intended to change God's mind?

Lk 18:9–14. The parable of the pharisee and the publican

In this parable as elsewhere we return to the idea of the kingdom as sheer gift. It is important for understanding this parable to realise that the pharisee in the story really was a very good and pious man. He had committed no mortal sins and his behaviour was scrupulously religious. He really did fast twice a week and tithe his possessions. His motivations, however, were all wrong; all his high religious and moral standards merely fed his self-love. The publican on the other hand knew that he was spiritually and morally bankrupt; he was excommunicated, a traitor to his country and his faith, openly exploiting other people, rejected in every sort of decent society. He knew that he had no claim on God's mercy and because of this he was capable of repentance and was capable of receiving the kingdom, the kingdom which is only received by the poor in spirit.

How do we avoid the danger of thanking God that we are not like the pharisee?

Lk 18:15–17. Jesus and the children (Mk 10:13–16; Mt 9:13–15)

This episode makes a similar point. To receive the kingdom we have to become like little children. We have to have the poverty of spirit which we normally associate with children. Acceptance of the kingdom must be based on childlike simplicity rather than any illusions about our own lovableness, or good qualities.

Lk 18:18–25. The rich ruler (Mk 10:17–31; Mt 19:16–30)

The main character in this episode does not have the advantages of the publican or the children. Although the advice Jesus gives to the young man is an individual challenge he goes on to enunciate a general principle which goes far beyond what we used to regard as an evangelical council of perfection. All men are called to perfection, and the second Vatican council has reminded us that we are all in varying degrees called to practise the counsels of poverty, chastity and obedience according to our individual situation and state of life. The point of the gospel passage is not that riches are in themselves bad, it is not even that the rich man is being invited to have compassion on the poor, the real point is that money causes a man to have a false view of himself (cf Lk 12:15, a man's life does not consist in the abundance of his possessions). The real objection to riches and to material possessions in general is not that material things are bad but that too many of them numb our sense of real need.

Do you think that it is especially difficult to be a christian in the consumer society in which we live?

Lk 18:31–34. The third prediction of the passion (Mk 10:32–34; Mt 20:17–19)

Luke leaves out Mark's introduction to these verses (Mk 10:32). Again Jesus identifies the role of the Son of Man with that of the suffering servant. The disciples are blind to his meaning, as blind as the blind man of Jericho in the next section. Only after the resurrection will they understand the full import of his words (cf 24:26 f and 45 f).

Lk 18:35–19:10. The blind man of Jericho (Mk 10:46–52 and Mt 20:29–34)

The healing of the blind man (34–43) is interesting chiefly for the title 'Son of David' which the beggar uses to address Jesus. It is as the 'Son of David' that Jesus gives him sight. There are a number of similarities between this episode and the incident with Zacchaeus. Like the beggar, Zacchaeus is an outsider and this is reflected physically in both cases by the difficulty of reaching Jesus through the crowd. In both cases Jesus stops and addresses himself to the man; and in both cases the grace of the kingdom reaches out and heals. Despite his profession, Zacchaeus is an Israelite (verse 9) and his repentance illustrates the mission of the messiah to the outsider.

How might christians occupy themselves more with outsiders in parish, college, school, locality or place of work?

Lk 19:11–27. The parable of the pounds

It has been suggested that there are two parables mixed up here. The first, the parable of the pounds, is similar to Matthew's parable of the talents (Mt 25 : 14–30). This parable may be followed if the reader ignores verses 14 and 27. Originally this parable would have referred to the use made of God's gifts by the teachers and lawyers of Israel. The coming of the messiah would involve them in giving an account of their success or failure. Later this parable would have been adapted to refer to the readiness of the individual christian for the second coming. The other parable of 'the nobleman who went into a far country' is probably based on Archelaus' visit to Rome after the death of his father Herod the Great in 4 BC.

Despite the machinations of Archelaus' opponents, Augustus confirmed Archelaus as ruler and he returned to execute a bloody pogrom on his opponents. This item of contemporary history could be understood as a symbol of avenging judgement. In this composite passage, however, the parable becomes a more detailed allegory. Christ replaces Archelaus and the plotters become Jesus' opponents among the Jewish people ('his citizens').

Does the censure on the man who buried his talent have any relevance to the attitude of the church to its mission? Does it have any relevance to the inward-looking mentality of much institutional christianity?

5

The Jerusalem ministry
Lk 19:28–21:38

Lk 19:28–40. The entry into Jerusalem (Mk 11:1–11; Mt 21:1–11; Jn 12:12–19)

Luke omits the detail of the palms being strewn in the road. Like the episode of the transfiguration, the entry into Jerusalem is clearly intended to fulfil Zechariah's vision of the coming of the messiah as the perfect fulfilment of the feast of tabernacles. Some scholars have even suggested that the triumphal entry into Jerusalem did not take place at the passover at all, but at some earlier date when Jesus and his disciples had gone up to Jerusalem for the feast of tabernacles. If this was the case then we can see how much greater dramatic effect was gained by placing it at the beginning of Holy Week and setting it in such sharp contrast with the other confrontation between the crowd and the messiah on Good Friday.

A triumphant entry into the ancient city of David at a major feast on an ass in deliberately contrived fulfilment of Zech 9:9, all amounted to a quite unequivocal claim by Jesus to be the messiah. Not only this, but the proceedings amounted to a very successful political demonstration. Everybody in the crowd now expected Jesus to lead a movement of political liberation from the Romans. The lament over Jerusalem which follows (41–44) is peculiar to Luke. That Jesus should have

responded to such a tumultuous welcome with the com-
plaint that Jerusalem did not know the time of her
visitation (44) is a little surprising. The real point is that
they had mistaken the real purpose of his coming. A prediction of the fall of Jerusalem could not have been
further from their nationalistic minds.

In fulfilment of Mal 3:1–3 Jesus then enters the
temple and provokes a direct confrontation with the religious establishment. Luke omits any reference to any
of Jesus' more violent actions on this occasion.

*1. Would Jesus have more or less significance for his-
tory if he had allowed himself to have been made the
leader of a nationalist movement?*

*2. Does Jesus' refusal to become a nationalistic messiah
necessarily suggest that christians should not support
revolutionary movements today?*

Lk 20:1–8. The day of questions: a question on authority (Mk 11:27–33; Mt 21:23–27)

This is the first of four questions posed on the 'day of
questions' (verses 1–47). Luke's account follows Mark's
fairly closely although in Luke the question on authority
follows immediately on the episode of the cleansing of
the temple, and thus gives a special poignancy to the
question. The fact that it is the 'chief priests, and the
scribes with the elders' emphasises that this is a continuation of the confrontation between Jesus and the entire
religious establishment of the temple. The question is
intended to entrap Jesus. Either he must publicly proclaim himself messiah under the very nose of the Roman
governor and risk almost certain arrest, or else he must
be seen to climb down before the ecclesiastical authorities. Jesus' answer is not just an evasion. John had recog-

nised Jesus as the messiah (chapter three) and if they believed in the mission of John as the prophesied fore-runner then they would be able to recognise the true character of Jesus' mission also. In fact of course they had carefully avoided committing themselves about John. Like all leaders of institutional religion they were ex-tremely wary about anything so undisciplined and free of ecclesiastical control as prophecy. On the other hand John had a very considerable popular following and they were reluctant to risk popular outrage by publicly dis-avowing him (5).

Why do priests tend to feel uncomfortable about pro-phets? Are the priests always in the wrong in having this attitude?

Lk 20:9–19. The day of questions: the wicked tenants (Mk 12:1–12 and Mt 21:33–46)

The parable which follows represents the second blow by Jesus in his battle of words with the religious authori-ties. The image of Israel as a vineyard originated with Is 5:1–7 ('My beloved had a vineyard on a very fruitful hill. He digged it . . . and planted it . . . the vineyard of the Lord of Hosts is the house of Israel, and the men of Judah are his pleasant planting; and he looked for justice but behold, bloodshed . . .'). The religious leaders of Israel are like dishonest tenants who refuse to accept their master's claims. The whole history of Israel had been marked by the persecution of the prophets and would be capped by the killing of the Son. God's judgement on them would result in the destruction of Jerusalem and the opening up of the treasures of judaism to gentiles and outsiders. It is doubtful whether this detailed inter-pretation was implied in the earliest forms of the parable.

Each of the three synoptic writers tried to reinforce the moral of the story more strongly. In common with Matthew, Luke pushes allegory one stage further by having the son murdered outside the vineyard (verse 15), like Jesus being crucified outside Jerusalem (Heb 13:12, 'So Jesus also suffered outside the gate'). On other points Luke's version only differs from Mark's over the number and fate of the messengers. Verse 17 is a quotation from Ps 118 and demonstrates the clear connection which exists between the death and resurrection of Jesus. Either Jesus or the evangelist is unable to end the parable on the note of death and retribution. The interruption by the audience in verse 16 is found only in Luke. Verse 18 seems oddly out of place here and it seems likely that Luke has introduced it here simply as another saying using the stone metaphor.

Do you agree that the death of Christ has too often been spoken of in complete isolation from the resurrection?

Lk 20:20–26. The day of questions: questions on tribute to Caesar (Mk 12:13–17; Mt 22:15–22)

Unlike Mark, Luke does not specify that the spies are Herodians and pharisees. Their intention is the same as in the question on authority in verse two; to provide Jesus with the opportunity to publicly compromise himself with the Roman authorities. If, on the other hand, he were to support the payment of the poll tax he would lose much of his popular support. Jesus manages to compromise his opponents without committing himself to either rebellion or collaboration. The image of Caesar on the denarius made the coinage technically idolatrous; by using the hated coinage and even bringing it into the temple his opponents had shown that their consciences were not really so tender after all. The pronouncement in verse 25 has been used down the centuries to justify the development of the so-called 'two kingdoms' theory, whereby everything to do with politics and economics is regarded as being within Caesar's province and God has all too often been left with religion, private (largely sexual) morality, and the hereafter. In fact Jesus leaves us with the unanswered question of what can rightly be labelled Caesar's and what labelled God's. His opponents had already decided their position on the question of currency. Within their terms the money belonged to Caesar, but the wider question remains.

1. Should christians pay their taxes when they know that some of their money will be used for immoral purposes (eg nuclear weapons)?

2. Did the second Vatican council do right in recognising the right of conscientious objection?

3. Should priests and bishops openly identify with political movements?

4. Are the churches too compromised to witness against the injustices in modern society?

Lk 20:27-40. The day of questions: question about the resurrection (Mk 12:18-27, Mt 22:23-33)

Up to verse 33 Luke follows Mark's version of the episode. The sadducees accepted only the authority of the five books of Moses, the *torah,* and they rejected the later beliefs in good and evil spirits and in the resurrection of the dead. The *torah* specified that a man should marry his dead brother's wife so as to give his brother legal descendants (Deut 25:5–10). By producing this absurd speculation they hoped to use the authority of the *torah* to disprove the pharisaic teaching on the resurrection. Luke's version of Jesus' reply brings out the fatuity of the question. There is no marriage in the final resurrection because there is no more death (36) and thus no necessity for heirs. The 'sons of the resurrection' will be like the angels that the sadducees do not believe in. Although belief in the resurrection was a late development in the history of the Jewish people Jesus refers back to Moses' encounter with Yahweh in the burning bush (Ex 3:6) 'where he calls the Lord the God of Abraham and the God of Isaac and the God of Jacob'. If the living God was God to these long dead patriarchs then they must have been alive: 'for all live to him.'

1. Is there any reason to believe in life after death except as a consequence of a relationship of faith in the living God? How convincing do you find arguments for immortality based only on natural reason?

2. Do you find christian teaching too preoccupied with life after death?

Lk 20:41–44. David's son (Mk 12:35–37 and Mt 22:41–45)

Jesus now poses a question himself. Presupposing, as he did, that Moses was the author of all the psalms, Jesus quotes the first verse of psalm 110 as the words of David himself. On David's own authority the messiah is rather more than a simple successor of David. The title 'Son of David', then, does not exhaust the concept of the messiah whom David addresses as 'Lord'. Apart from the words 'Book of Psalms' in verse 42, Luke follows Mark exactly in this passage.

Does the fact that Jesus was almost certainly wrong about the authorship of the psalm in question undermine the real message of these verses? Does it create problems for those of us who believe in the divinity of Christ?

Lk 20:45–21:4. True and false piety (Mk 12:38–44)

Luke continues following the Marcan order in these verses, where he provides a vivid contrast between the bogus religiosity of the scribes and the wholehearted goodness of the poor widow. Here as elsewhere the emphasis is upon Jesus reversing the world's verdict on outward piety and the value of money.

1. Do clergymen sometimes get more respect shown to them than is good for them? In our sort of society is it spiritually dangerous for priests, bishops and religious to wear distinctive clothing; to be called 'Father', 'My Lord', 'Reverend' etc? Do you think Jesus Christ would have approved of the custom of money being paid for priests to say masses for a special intention? Try to give fair attention to any contrary arguments.

2. What proportion of a person's income should be donated to worthy causes? Do the institutional churches spend too much breath and effort on trying to raise money? Can this be blamed on lack of lay generosity? How much control should the laity have in deciding how money is to be spent before they are asked to support church funds?

Lk 21:5–36. The apocalyptic teaching (Mk 13:1–32 and Mt 24:1–36)

This section consists of groups of sayings about the destruction of the temple, the siege of Jerusalem and the second coming of Christ. A large part of the section

follows closely Mk 13, but there are a number of specifically
Lucan elements which have been added. Luke's account
seems to be taking more cognisance of the actual events
of the siege of Jerusalem in AD 70, thus suggesting to
some scholars that Luke's gospel was written after this
date, and there is a clear attempt to soften the force of
Jesus' teaching on the imminence of the second coming.

Luke 21 : 5–19. Jesus is prophesying the destruction of
the temple and in Luke he makes this prophecy, suitably
enough, in the temple rather than on the Mount of Olives
as in Mark. Mark (13:3) has the inner group of Peter,
James, Andrew and John asking 'when these things are
all to be accomplished'. 'These things' is clearly a reference to more than just the destruction of Jerusalem.
Luke's purpose throughout this passage is to minimise the
connection between the local events of the destruction of
the temple and the city of Jerusalem and the cosmic
catastrophe of the final judgement and the second coming. Luke's version, therefore, reads 'when will this be?'.
Verses 7–11 follow Mark fairly closely although the
words 'then he said to them' in verse 10 are not found in
Mark. Verses 11–13, however, provide a very differently
expressed version of the Marcan verses and Luke is here
clearly drawing from his own special source. In verse 13
Luke replaces Mk 13:10 'the gospel must first be preached
to all nations' because by the time Luke is writing it had
already reached Rome, the centre of the world.

Luke 21 : 20–35: The siege of Jerusalem. A comparison between verse 20 and Mk 10:14 reinforces the
impression of a later date for Luke's gospel. Mark's sac-
rilege in the temple has been replaced by Luke's sur-
rounding armies. Verse 22 also is peculiar to Luke. In
verse 24 Luke gives more detailed information of the
events following the fall of Jerusalem. After the carnage

and the captivity there will be the time of the gentiles, the period of unspecified length between the fall of Jerusalem and the final judgement (cf Dan 12:7). The cosmic catastrophes of verses 25–28 will be God's judgement on the gentiles in their turn. The fig tree in verse 29 is the parable of the impending end. The signs are unmistakable. In Mark it is the Son of Man who is indicated by these signs, but in Luke it is 'the kingdom of God'. Verse 32 has presented biblical scholars with problems for a very long time. In its original context in Mk 13 : 31 it may be a genuine saying of Jesus indicating his mistaken belief that the parousia will follow within a generation. Alternatively this verse may be seen as referring back to the earlier statements about the destruction of the temple and the city of Jerusalem. Clearly Mark, writing much earlier, associated these local events with the coming end. However, it is much more likely that Luke was understanding them as referring only to the destruction of Jerusalem. Another line of interpretation of this verse would refuse to understand the word 'generation' literally but see it as representing the period between the death and resurrection of Christ and his second coming. Whichever of these interpretations is correct the lesson of verses 34 to 36 is clear enough. The disciple must practise vigilance and be ready for the second coming at any time.

1. How possible is it for us to regard military reverses like the destruction of a city as the work of God?

2. Why is it that christians have so often seen the kingdom in terms of individual salvation in another world?

3. Would it matter if Christ were wrong about the precise time of his second coming? Would it matter if Mark or Luke was wrong?

6

The passion narrative
Lk 22:1–23:56

Lk 22:1–6. Plot and betrayal. (Mk 14:1–12 and Mt 26:1–16)

The Jewish historian Josephus shared Mark and Luke's apparent confusion of the feast of passover with the feast of unleavened bread. The passover was the great commemoration of the exodus; the liberation of the Israelites from slavery in Egypt. This festival would be celebrated by the solemn public sacrifices of the paschal lambs in the temple commemorating the first paschal lamb which, according to Ex 12:21–27, was slaughtered and used for the smearing of the doorposts of each Israelite home in Egypt on the night on which the angel of death killed the first-born of the Egyptians. Observing the blood, the angel 'passed over' their homes and reserved his terrors for their enemies. The feast of unleavened bread, or the feast of Omer, took place on the day after the main passover festival and was an agricultural feast celebrating the harvesting of the first sheaf of barley.

The plotting of the scribes and the chief priests and the defection and treachery of Judas set the stage for the slaughter of a new passover lamb; the messiah-liberator himself. Luke follows Mark in these verses but he leaves out Mk 14:2 'Not during the feast, lest there be a tumult of the people'. This was a logical piece of tidying up as all of the synoptic gospels represent Jesus as suffering on the feast of passover itself. He also leaves out Mark's account of the anointing in Bethany, perhaps because of its similarities with the incident in chapter 7.

Luke ignores possible reasons for Judas' betrayal of Jesus: 'Satan entered into' him. John attributes Judas' treachery to simple greed. Other speculations have included suggestions that Judas was one of the militant zealots disillusioned with the non-violent line Jesus appeared to be taking, and trying to put him to the test one way or the other. But neither Luke nor the other evangelists exhibit much interest in the psychology of the man whose name has become a synonym for double-dyed treachery. More important to them is the importance of Judas as an instrument in God's plan (see verse 22). Some, admittedly rather off-beat, christians have even venerated him as a saint, obviously not for his personal qualities but because of the importance of his role in the drama of man's redemption.

In many ways Judas exemplifies a very serious problem about God's dealings with man. If the man was cast in the role of traitor from the beginning then was not his freedom in some way limited?

Lk 22:7–21. The upper room. (Mk 14:12–36 and Mt 26:17–29)

Only Luke gives the names of the disciples mentioned in verse 8. The previous verse combines with the second part of verse 8 to suggest that the meal which is to be the last supper for Jesus and the disciples is to be the passover meal, the intimate family gathering which followed the public sacrifices in the temple. In fact this is one of the most vexed problems of biblical scholarship and need not detain us here. Sufficient to say that if the last supper was not the passover meal as such then it was at least intended as an anticipation of it and it was intended to show Jesus as the fulfilment of the feast. To 'make ready for the passover' would involve buying the paschal lamb, and after its ritual slaughter in the temple, cooking it. Unleavened bread, bitter herbs, and wine would also be needed. Mark begins the passover meal with the prophecy of betrayal but Luke leaves it over until the conclusion of the meal.

The two cups in verses 17 and 20 present another major problem for scholars. Many, though by no means the majority, of manuscripts leave out the second part of verse 19 and the whole of verse 20. Was the cup in verse 17 the same cup as in Mk 14 : 22? Either Luke has preserved another, possibly earlier, tradition which later scribes have supplemented with the words of Paul in 1 Cor 11 (the only other account of the Lord's words which include the specific command that the eucharist is to be repeated) or else the writers of the other manuscripts have been misled into thinking that Luke has repeated himself and left out the second cup. If the last supper was a passover meal, then the first cup presents no problem since the passover included no less than four cups of wine. Obviously a highly technical critical problem is not going to be resolved in a discussion group but it is both profitable and interesting to notice the difference of emphasis between the two cups. The first cup, like the passover itself, (see 22 : 16–17) looks forward to the future, to the manifestation of the kingdom. Verses 19 and 20 emphasise the eucharist as a looking back, a 'remembrance', like the passover itself. The Greek word for remembrance (*anamnesis*) has greater depths than are obvious from the

English word. 'Remembrance' here involves the idea not only of past events being recalled to the mind but of being made in some mysterious way present, and the words 'do'_and 'remembrance' both have sacrificial connotations. The eucharist is a passover meal that makes the saving events of the past available in the present. It is also a meal which, like the passover, anticipates a final messianic banquet in the future.

1. Have christians lost sight of the eucharist as a promise of a future liberation? If so does it matter?

2. What common ground is there between those who regard the eucharist as a commemorative meal and those who believe that it is a sacrifice?

3. In what ways can the celebration of the eucharist today take into account all the longing for liberation and a better future which exists among so many of the young, the coloured and the poor? Has the social and political dimension of the eucharist been neglected?

Lk 22:21–38. Discourse after the last supper (Mk 14:17–31; Mt 26:20–35)

Verses 21–23 are an abbreviated version of Mk 14:18–21, where they precede the supper. By placing them at this point Luke makes Judas' presence at the supper more plausible, as it is scarcely likely that he would have stayed on after hearing these words. Their position here also makes the point to the early christians that participation in the eucharist is no guarantee against apostasy and betrayal.

The controversy of verses 24–30 is treated much earlier in the gospel story in Mark and Matthew. Perhaps Luke was influenced in this by his understanding of the eucharist as a sign of the coming kingdom. Jesus' role as a waiter to the disciples at the last supper provides a model of what authority and ministry will mean in the community of the kingdom (22:27, 'I am among you as one who serves'). The disciples will indeed share in the royal authority of the messiah in the future kingdom (22:28–30) but it will not be authority on the secular model of domination; the only primacy in the kingdom will be primacy of service.

In view of the role that Luke records for Peter in the early chapters of Acts it is hardly surprising that Luke includes a saying about Peter here. The man who was to have a very real primacy of service would first have to cope with a terrible trial of strength in which he would be found wanting. But with the prediction of Peter's denials there is the commission to be a special strength to the early church.

The instructions about the swords are found only in Luke and are usually taken to be meant ironically. Unlike the time of the mission of the seventy-two (10:4) the hey-day of public support is now over. Whatever else must be expected public opposition is now certain. Perhaps Jesus was also seeking to identify symbolically with the liberator expected by the zealots, but if the words had been meant literally two swords would scarcely have constituted an adequate arsenal. The medieval understanding of the two swords as an allegory for political and spiritual power, both committed to the successors of Peter, is almost a parody of Jesus' teaching in verses 24–27.

1. It has been said that 'the mantle of the Caesars fell on the shoulders of the fisherman'; do you think that the papacy ever emerges clearly as spiritual authority based on service rather than a centre for the domination of the human spirit?

2. *How far can our Lord's teaching on authority and service be implemented by simply reflecting upon it at an* individual *level, and how far must the whole role of the clergy be reassessed and changed at a* structural *level?*

Lk 22:39–46. The agony in the garden (Mk 14:26, 32–42 and Mt 26:30, 36–46)

Luke's version of this episode is very different from that found in Mark. Luke does not call the garden Gethsemane, but simply 'the Mount of Olives'. 'The disciples' replace Peter, James, and John, and they are asked to pray, not as a gesture of solidarity with Jesus in his trial but 'that they may not enter into temptation'. Their failure in this is somewhat kindly interpreted as being due to grief (22 : 45) and the severe rebuke found in Mark is not repeated here. Luke and Matthew both show much greater respect for the apostles than the author of Mark's gospel and this is a very good instance of the tendency in Luke. Verses 43–44 are peculiar to Luke and emphasise the extreme anguish and psychological dereliction which Jesus must have experienced. Not surprisingly some manuscripts omit these two verses since they portray Jesus at his most human.

Do christians still tend to underestimate the humanity of Christ?

Lk 22:47–23:5. The arrest and trial of Jesus (Mk 14:43–15:5 and Mt 26:47–27:14; cf Jn 18:2–38)

Luke's account of the arrest of Jesus differs from Mark's in a number of details. He does not tell us that Judas actually kissed Jesus or that he called him 'master' but Jesus' poignant question to Judas: 'would you betray the Son of Man with a kiss?' is found only in Luke, and only Luke supplies us with the detail of the healing of the high priest's slave's ear. The second half of verse 53 suggests to the reader that just as Judas' betrayal was part of the plan of God so the forces at work behind the scenes in the arrest of Jesus are part of some great drama in which the cosmic power of evil is temporarily in control of the situation.

All of the other evangelists represent the denial of Jesus by Peter as taking place before the beginning of the trial before Annas and Caiaphas. Again Luke alone has certain features which make it a much more vivid account. The maid looks at Peter 'as he sat in the light'; after the three denials 'the Lord turned and looked at Peter'; and 'he went out and wept bitterly'. The mocking of Jesus takes place before the trial in Luke and his tormentors here are not the sanhedrin but the temple guards. Luke omits the spitting of Mk 14:65 but makes sense out of the covering of his head in the same verse by linking it with the taunt 'prophesy'. The first trial of Jesus, by the sanhedrin, now follows but in keeping with the other alterations in the Marcan order Luke has this episode taking place in the morning rather than during the night. The sanhedrin consisted of the council of 'elders . . . priests and scribes' who made up the ruling synod of the Jewish faith, which shared authority with the chief priest. They press him to make some messianic claim which they can interpret as heretical and the prophecy in verse 69 provides them with all they need. But they are unwilling to pass sentence themselves, although according to some historians they may well have had the authority to do so. The execution of Stephen in Acts 7 need not necessarily reflect any change in the law on the subject since the death of Christ. By putting the ball squarely in the Roman governor's court they effectively provided an alternative target for any popular outrage at the crucifixion. Pilate's question in verse 3 and the charge that Jesus is a political troublemaker in verse 5 (both verses are peculiar to Luke) make it clear that the charge being brought is now one of sedition rather than blasphemy. Pilate would not, after all, be very interested in the theological niceties of Jewish messianism.

If Pilate had understood the true role of the messiah do you agree that he would have considered Jesus to be politically harmless? Would the subsequent history of the Roman Empire have justified this assumption?

Lk 23:8–25. Trial before Herod and second trial before Pilate. (Mk 15:6–15 and Mt 27:15–26; cf Jn 18:38–19:16)

The trial before Herod is not found in any other gospel. If it is historical then Luke may have had access to this information through a possible acquaintance with Manaen, 'a member of the court of Herod the Tetrarch' (Acts 13 : 1) or through Joanna 'the wife of Chuza, Herod's steward' (Lk 8 : 3) whose name is not given in any of the other gospels. Whether or not it is a fabrication Luke's purpose in including it is clear from his use of Ps 2 : 2 in Acts 4 : 26, where Pilate and Herod become representative of the kings and rulers who 'were gathered together against the Lord and against his anointed'. In Luke's account the mockery of Jesus by Pilate's soldiers is replaced by the mocking in the court of Herod (23 : 11). The quarrel referred to in 23 : 12 is not otherwise known. Herod is represented as seeking a possible diversion from a performance by Jesus (23 : 8) but the silence of Jesus, modelled on the suffering servant who 'opened not his mouth' (Is 53 : 7), merely irritates Herod and he returns him to Pilate. Again (see 22 : 66) Luke emphasises that the death of Jesus is being sought by the entire Jewish religious establishment: 'the chief priests and the rulers and the people'. It is hard not to notice the extent to which Luke is concerned with playing down the guilt of the Romans in the whole affair and laying the major part of the blame on the Jewish leaders and the Jewish pilgrims as a whole. His personal involvement in the gentile mission and his reluctance to provoke the Romans may be partly the cause of this attitude. Verse 16 does not specify the cruel nature of the scourging and, like John, Luke represents this action as a palliative offer intended as an alternative to the exaction of the maximum penalty. In Mark and Matthew scourging is simply the routine preliminary to crucifixion. The name Barabbas means 'Son of the Father', and lends itself to fascinating speculations that Barabbas may have been some mysterious alter-ego of Jesus himself. The more pedestrian explanation, however, which Luke himself no doubt intended, was that a bogus, rather third-rate, guerrilla had been released in response to popular demand while the genuine messiah was condemned to death.

Do you agree that the role of the Jews in the passion narratives have played their part historically in the rise of anti-semitism? How can the narratives be taught in a way that avoids this danger?

Lk 23:26–32. The road to the cross. (Mk 15:20–23; Mt 27:31–34; cf Jn 19:17)

It was quite normal procedure for a condemned man to carry the *patibulum* or cross-piece of the cross to the place of execution. Presumably weakened by the ordeal of the trials and the watching of the night before, Jesus was unable to continue. A passing pilgrim is pressed into carrying the beam for him, and Simon becomes the representative figure for every follower of Jesus who responds to the challenge of Lk 14:27. Luke omits the detail in Mark that Simon was the father of Alexander and Rufus.

There is a measure of ambiguity in the role both of the women of Jerusalem and of the good thief. We may take both as being completely sincere or we may discern an ambivalence in their attitude. In the case of the women their mourning may have been purely a ritualised, conventional mourning. Genuine or not, Jesus observes their expressions of grief and tells them that they would do better to reserve their sorow for their own plight when his prophecies about the destruction of Jerusalem are fulfilled (23:28). Barrenness was always accounted a terrible disgrace among Jewish woman, but even this shame would be preferable to the dreadful events which would follow (23:29). If the terrible suffering of an innocent man which they were witnessing could happen at this time, 'when the wood is green' what much worse sufferings would happen in the time of the gentiles, 'when it is dry' (23:31), a reference to the war of 66–70. This episode of the women of Jerusalem, like the reference to the criminals being led out with him of verse 32, is found only in Luke.

1. Do you agree that it would be more difficult to dismiss christianity as a narcotic for the inadequate and the fearful if Simon was more frequently regarded as the model for following Christ?

2. *It could be argued that certain types of traditional christian devotions involve the worshipper in 'feeling sorry' for Jesus in a rather sentimental and even psychologically sick fashion. Can you offer any comments on such arguments?*

Lk 23:33–39. Jesus on the cross (1). (Mk 15:22–41, Mt 27:33–56; cf Jn 19:17–30)

Luke omits the place name *Golgotha* which is given in Mark and Matthew. Instead he gives the Greek translation, in English, 'the skull'. The word 'Calvary' derives from the Latin *calvaria,* meaning skull. That Jesus suffered with criminals was a conscious reference to his role of the suffering servant of Is 53:12: 'he poured out his soul to death, and was numbered with the transgressors.' Only Luke gives us the 'Father, forgive them'. It is quite typical of Luke that he should place this extreme emphasis upon the mercy of the messiah and the way in which his kingdom always reaches out beyond the barriers erected by men. Not surprisingly, this verse was left out of some manuscripts, almost certainly by some scribe who found the idea of Jesus forgiving the Jews rather too much to swallow. The prayer for forgiveness could be taken as a prayer for the Romans but, while they are no doubt to be included as well it is very unlikely that Jesus would have wished to exclude the sanhedrin and others who were the real instigators of the crime. Read in conjunction with the prayer of Stephen in Acts 7:60 and with the teaching of Acts 3:17 and 13:27, this interpretation becomes quite certain.

The sharing out of the garments (23:34) and the

mocking (23:35–36) are both echoes of Ps 22:7, 18, while the taunt of the rulers in verse 35 is strongly reminiscent of the taunt against the just man who is condemned 'to a shameful death' in Wis 2:12–20. In Mk 15:29–30 the taunt was that Jesus had claimed to be able to destroy and rebuild the temple in three days. Here the taunt hinges on another alleged claim; that he was king of the Jews.

Why have christians so often used the death of Christ as an excuse for persecuting the Jews?

Lk 23:39–43. Jesus on the cross (2)

The episode of the conversation with the repentant thief in 39–43, based on the second half of Mk 15:32, is found only in Luke and this is consistent with the emphasis of the gospel as the 'outsiders' gospel': a common thief hanging on a gibbet was doubly damned according to the teaching of the Pentateuch (see Deut 21:22–23). We may either take the thief's request as meant and constituting a real affirmation of faith in Christ or we may regard the words as 'gently ironic, a courageous jest which the Lord takes up seriously' (Leaney). The word 'paradise' in 23:43 involves another ambiguity. The roots of the Greek word suggest a park or garden with all the obvious associations with the garden of Eden. This provides an image both for the final kingdom, glorious like its mythical beginning, and also for that part of the underworld (*Sheol*) reserved for the just who were awaiting the general resurrection. Either the thief is being promised a place in the new Eden of the kingdom, which is to come as a consequence of the death of Christ, or else he is being offered access to an other-worldly happiness which may await the individual beyond the grave.

*Does belief in personal survival beyond the grave help
or hinder in the struggle to improve conditions in this
world?*

Lk 23:44–49. Jesus dies on the cross. (Mk 15:33–41; Mt 27:45–56; Jn 19:25–30)

The fact that passover was celebrated at full moon makes
it quite impossible that verse 45 can be a reference to a
historical eclipse. If it did happen it must have been pure
miracle. The point of the sun's light failing, however, is
to establish a link between the coming of the messianic
age and the perturbation of the heavenly bodies already
referred to in chapter 21. In a very real sense the death
of Jesus and the day of judgement are the same event. All
men are now judged by their response to the cross. The
rending of the veil in verse 45 refers not only to the tear-
ing down of the literal veil which screened off the most
sacred area of the temple, it is also a most eloquent symbol of the breaking down of every barrier between man
and God. The whole of the epistle to the Hebrews is an
elaboration of this theme: 'we have confidence to enter
the sanctuary by the blood of Jesus, by the new and living
way which he opened for us through the curtain, that is
through his flesh.' (Heb 10 : 19–20). Other more recent
commentators have seen the torn veil as the destruction
in Christ of the whole 'religious' approach to God. For
the christian there can no longer be the anxious, guilt-
ridden attitude to the holy which so often results in the
attempt to restrict God to the temple and keep religion
divorced from real life.

Verse 46 leaves out Mark's despairing cry from Jesus
(15 : 34), perhaps because some might have mistakenly regarded it as a culpable lack of confidence in God. In its

place Luke details the unspecified cry of Mk 15:37: 'Father, into thy hands I commend my spirit'; a quotation from Ps 31:5. Luke has also changed the exclamation of the centurion in 23:47. Mark has 'this man was the Son of God' but in Luke the emphasis is on the much repeated theme of the innocence of Jesus. Only Luke tells us of the repentant attitude of the crowd and it is likely that this detail was based on the prophecy in Zech 12:10: 'when they look on him whom they have pierced, they shall mourn for him as one mourns for an only child.' Verse 49 has strong echoes of Ps 28:12 and Ps 88:9.

Do you agree that many christians have attempted to mend the veil of the temple in order to minimise the impact of the gospel upon real life? Is it a mistake to have sacred buildings at all? Do you know of any ways in which attempts have been made to 'desacralise' the mass? Is this a desirable aim?

Lk 23:50–56. The burial of Jesus. (Mk 15:42–47; Mt 27:57–61; cf Jn 19:38–42)

All four gospels record the role of Joseph of Arimathea, although the whereabouts of Arimathea is not known. He was a member of the sanhedrin but was not implicated in the condemnation of Jesus. Like Simeon and Anna in chapter 2, Joseph is one of those who 'was looking for the kingdom of God' although in John's gospel Joseph is an actual disciple of Jesus (19:38). Luke leaves out the details of the conversation with Pilate (Mk 15:44–45) and his questioning of the centurion. The details follow of the new tomb, the linen shroud and the inspection of the tomb by the very women who were to be the first witnesses of the resurrection. The 'day of preparation' referred to in verse 54 is a reference not to the eve of the passover but to the eve of the sabbath which always began at dusk on the Friday night.

1. Do you think that the commemoration of the death and burial of Jesus on Good Friday is a good idea? Might it possibly suggest to people that Jesus was somehow dead all over again instead of being always present as the living, risen Christ?

2. Can you see any continuing purpose or usefulness in the erection of gravestones and monuments or the existence of cemeteries? Do they help us to see any characteristically christian attitude to death?

7

The resurrection of Jesus
Lk 24:1–53

**Lk 24: 1–12. The women at the tomb. (Mk 16: 1–8;
Mt 28: 1–10; cf Jn 20: 1–18)**
The 'first day of the week' has always been celebrated by
the church as the day of the resurrection. This has to be
seen against the background of the seven 'days' of creation
in Gen 1. The eighth day, the first day of the new week,
marks the beginning of the new creation. The old order
has been both fulfilled and replaced. The women who
came to embalm the body of Jesus are not named here
but the list of their names has already been given in
verse 10. On their arrival at the tomb they find it empty.
Luke is at great pains here to emphasise that they did
actually search for the body. The words 'of the Lord
Jesus' are the first of a number of phrases in Luke–Acts
which are not found in one important family of
manuscripts: the Western, or Old Latin, text and the
Codex Bezae. In each case these phrases and verses were
probably not in the original gospel and they are not included in the text by the editors of the Revised Standard
Version or the New English Bible. Later additions or not,
catholic tradition regards them as canonical and they have
been restored to the text in the catholic edition of the
Revised Standard Version.
Only Luke says that there were 'two men' standing by

the tomb. Mark mentions only one man; Matthew one angel, and John two angels. It is of course just possible that Luke is treating the terms 'angel' and 'man' as interchangeable here in the same way as they are in Acts 10 : 3 (cf Acts 10 : 30). There are a number of points in the narrative, however, which suggest that the whole account is closely modelled on the account of the transfiguration of Jesus in Lk 9 : 31. If this is correct then it is at least plausible that the two men, both here and in Acts 1 : 10 are really intended to represent Moses and Elijah as the representatives of the law and the prophets, both fulfilled in the resurrection and exaltation of Christ. The first part of 24 : 6: 'He is not here, but has risen' is another one of the phrases not found in all the best manuscripts. The rest of the verse is a deliberate alteration of the Marcan 'he is going before you to Galilee.' As with the fourth gospel, Luke has no mention of any resurrection appearances in Galilee, since 'Luke is determined that the gospel shall start from Jerusalem and nowhere else' (Leaney; cf Acts 1 : 8). Verse 7 is reminiscent of the various foretellings of his passion by Jesus earlier in the gospel (9: 18–21, 44; 17 : 25; 18 : 31–33). The 'sinful men' referred to in this verse are the Romans; men outside the scope of the law. The calmness of the women in verse 9 is in sharp contrast with the terrified silence of the women in Mk 16 : 9: 'they said nothing . . . for they were afraid'. Verse 12 is another disputed verse which may have been included so as to harmonise Luke's account with that of Jn 20 : 3–10.

1. Do the discrepancies between the different accounts of the resurrection appearances make the resurrection less credible for us today? What do you think about those christians who assert that their faith in the truth of the resurrection would be unaffected even if the bones of Jesus were discovered somewhere in Palestine?

2. Is it reasonable of Roman catholic scholars to insist on retaining verses which may not have been present in the original text?

Lk 24: 13–35. The walk to Emmaus

This incident is found only in Luke, though it is mentioned in the longer ending of Mark (Mk 16:12–13). The two disciples on the road were not members of the inner circle of the twelve, and they can be regarded as representatives of the much wider circle of Jesus' followers. Cleopas has often been associated with the Clopas of Jn 19:25 and according to the church father Eusebius he was Jesus' uncle. There is some dispute about the site of Emmaus. It might have been the Emmaus where Judas Maccabeus destroyed the Macedonian camp (1 Mac 3:40 and 4:3) or it might have been the modern town of Kelonieh, four miles to the west of Jerusalem. The 'seven miles' of verse 13 is a very rough equivalent of the distance given in the Greek measurement of sixty *stades* (other manuscripts give the distance as one hundred and fifty *stades*. There are about eight *stades* to the mile). The extraordinary circumstance of their not recognising Jesus may be just a literary device to make the theological point that Jesus can only be known through the right understanding of the old testament scriptures (verse 27) and through participation in the eucharist (verse 35). 'Breaking of bread' is a common new testament expression for the Lord's supper (cf Acts 2:42, 46; 20:7, 11; 27:35 and 1 Cor 10:16). Verse 21 makes clear that they had abandoned all hope in Jesus' messianic mission. There was more than one sense in which they were unable to recognise him. The rebuke in verse 25 makes this clear. Lost in their nationalistic dreams of a free Zion they were quite incapable of making the necessary link-up in their minds between the conquering messiah and the suffering servant of Deutero-Isaiah. He then interprets for them the whole of the old testament as a salvation history which reaches its climax in the suffering and exaltation of the messiah (verse 27). In verse 30 they recognise him in the familiar action of breaking bread. He then disappears. Once they have realised that he is indeed risen and that he is present with them in word and sacrament they no longer need the person-to-person physical presence of a visible Jesus. The whole episode has been recorded in such a way as to make the maximum catechetical use of this aspect of the story.

1. Does this passage have any relevance for the christian who is tortured by doubt or anxiety?

2. Does the old testament still serve a useful purpose today in the task of teaching and witnessing to the resurrection? Are there any limits to its usefulness?

3. Do you agree with the view that some of the disagreements about the nature of Christ's presence in the eucharist have been due to a failure to realise that it is the risen Jesus who is present and not a dead or dying one?

Lk 24:33–53. Jesus appears to the eleven. (Jn 20:19–23)

Luke represents the appearance of Jesus to the eleven as taking place only an hour after the appearance to the two disciples on the way to Emmaus (24: 33). The reply of the eleven that Jesus 'has appeared to Simon' must be a reference to the appearance mentioned by Paul in 1 Cor 15:5. 'As they were saying this, Jesus suddenly appears. The second half of verse 36 and the whole of verse 40 are left out in the Western text and may have been added in order to reinforce the similarities between this passage and the episode recorded in Jn 20:19–24. Luke emphasises the concrete tangible quality of the risen body of the Lord. They are invited to touch him (24:39) and, reminiscent of the action of the angel in Tob 12:16–22, Jesus eats in front of them. No doubt this emphasis was intended to signify that the appearance of Jesus was not just a common subjective hallucination and it was intended to rule out any docetic tendency. (The docetists were early heretics who denied the real humanity of Christ and held that he was just the appearance of a man). In addition to the doctrinal and apologetic purpose Luke is also concerned to show the faith of the church is confirmed by the presence of the risen Christ eating with his followers in the Sunday eucharist. The discourse in 44–49 is very like verses 24–27 and foreshadows the structure of the argument which Peter is to use on the day of Pentecost (Acts 2). The proclamation of the death and resurrection of Jesus is directed towards producing repentance and the acceptance of God's forgiveness (47). This proclamation is to begin at Jerusalem and go out from there 'to all nations' and this process will begin with Jesus' gift of the Holy Spirit: 'the promise of the Father', prophesied by Joel, who was to be received on the day of Pentecost.

Verses 50–53 may or may not be an account of the ascension. If they are, then Luke, like John, sees the resurrection and the ascension as one event occurring on the same day (see Jn 20:17). However the words 'and was carried up into heaven' are omitted in the Western text and may have been added later simply to round off the ministry of Jesus in the same way as in the longer ending of Mark's gospel (Mk 16 : 19). Alternatively Luke himself may have written this shorter account of the ascension which he was able to take up again and amplify in Acts. The gospel ends in a way that takes us back to the beginning of the infancy narratives: it ends as it began in the temple at Jerusalem.

1. Is docetism still prevalent among christians today? If so, how does it manifest itself?

2. What meaning can we give to the ascension when we no longer think of heaven as a place in the sky?

Acts of the Apostles

Nicholas Lash

1

Foreword
Acts 1:1–11

Acts 1:1–5

As one might expect of 'volume two', Luke begins with
a summary of his first book. The elements that he chooses
for the summary are important, particularly the fact that
the proclamation of the kingdom is mentioned in the
context of the meals that Christ shared with the apostles
after his resurrection (cf RSV variant reading of 1 : 4). In
view of the importance given to these meals in the gospels (Lk 24 : 36–49), the readers of Acts will have grasped
the reference to their own situation: it is in the context
of the eucharist that the risen Lord speaks to his followers
of the kingdom. The 'founding' and 'manifestation' of
the kingdom through the agency of the Spirit (cf the
Vatican II *Constitution on the Church,* art 2) is a central
theme in Acts, which explains the fact that the Spirit is
mentioned twice in this prologue. The contrast between
christian baptism and the baptism of John (1 : 5) perhaps
has polemical undertones. The early church had to fight
to establish the radical difference between Jewish ritual
purification rites and the life-bearing Spirit-bath of baptism (11 : 16; 19 : 3; Mt 3 : 11; Mk 1 : 8). It is difficult to
reconcile the command to remain in Jerusalem (1 : 4)
with Matthew's account but, for Luke, this insistence on
Jerusalem has a threefold significance. In the first place,

his gospel is centred on Jerusalem, the focal point of the old dispensation. The action of the gospel both begins and ends in the temple at Jerusalem, the dwelling place of God among his people, and the middle section of the gospel is set in the form of a journey towards Jerusalem: the new dispensation flowers out of the old, and is its achievement (Lk 13 : 33–35). In the second place, the theme of Acts is the 'universalising' of the people of God in the new order of things, and Luke illustrates this by *beginning* the book in Jerusalem, capital city of the old, 'particular' people, and *ending* it in Rome, capital city of the known world. In the third place, in view of the fact that he is shortly going to describe the definitive out-pouring of the Spirit as taking place in Jerusalem, his insistence that the apostles *stay* in the city until the sending of the Spirit highlights the fact that it is only by the gift of the Spirit that the apostles are enabled to share in Christ's *teaching* mission (Jn 7 : 39; 16 : 13).

Is water-baptism 'in the name of Jesus' the same thing as 'baptism with the Holy Spirit'?

Acts 1:6–11

Luke begins his account of the ascension with a verse (1 : 6) which gives the impression of carrying on where the main narrative of the gospel left off (cf Lk 24 : 49). The question as to whether the closing verses of the gospel and the opening verses of Acts are the work of Luke or an 'unknown editor' is unresolved, probably insoluble, and not very important. The apostles' question shows such an undeveloped understanding of the nature of the kingdom that one cannot help wondering whether it is not simply a literary device (reminiscent of St John) to provide a contrast with the insistence, in the next two verses, on the universal kingdom manifested and achieved in the power of the Spirit.

Jesus is given the title 'Lord', reminding us that the earliest christian profession of faith consisted in the attribution of this divine title to the glorified Jesus (cf Phil 2 : 6–11; Is 45 : 23; Rom 10 : 9). The Lord's apparent refusal to answer the question 'when?' is a reminder that the establishment of the kingdom is the work of God alone (cf Dan 2 : 21; Mk 13 : 32). The second half of the answer (1 : 8) is a neat summary of the whole of Acts. It echoes Is 49 : 6; the image of the servant of Yahweh is never far from the mind of the early church (cf Is 42 : 1–9; 49 : 1–6; 50 : 4–11; 52 : 13–53 : 12).

Luke's account of the ascension can only be understood if we resist the modern tendency to carve up the paschal mystery into a series of separate 'events'. The death and glorification of Christ and the outpouring of the Spirit constitute *one* event, the salvation-event. In the johannine perspective, the death of Christ is already his glorification (cf Jn 17 : 1), and the sending of the apostles in the power of the Spirit is set in the context of Easter evening (cf Jn 20 : 21–22). The 'cloud' into which our Lord is assumed is the sign of the divine presence (cf Ex 13 : 22; 24 : 16–18). While there is an 'absence' of the Lord until his final coming (1 : 11; cf 1 Tim 3 : 16) which the community awaits in eager expectation, he is 'closer' during his 'absence' than he was in the days of his flesh (cf Mk 16 : 19–20). The task of the christian community is not to be sitting idle, 'gazing heavenward', but to be working, in the power of the Spirit, for the final 'coming', the achievement of the kingdom in God's own time.

1. Is the gift of the Spirit primarily for 'life' or 'witness'?

2. What practical difference would it make to our understanding and living of the christian faith if the phrase 'he ascended into heaven' were deleted from the creed?

2

The church at Jerusalem
Acts 1:12–5:42

Acts 1:12–26
This section serves as a bridge between the introduction
and the section on the church at Jerusalem (for which
Luke's principal source of information was quite probably Mark). As a summary of the life of the apostolic
community it should be compared with 2:42; 4:32–35,
and 5:12–16.

The number 120 was the minimum required to form
a legally recognised community in Jewish law. More important, it is a 'perfect number', symbolising the eschatological assembly of the people of God (cf Acts 7:1–8:
14): the complete and fulfilled community at the end of
time, when God is 'all in all'. As a 'complete' community,
the new Israel needs a 'complete' body of twelve leaders
(cf Mt 19:28). The college of 'the twelve', whose primary
function is that of witnessing to the resurrection, must
be made whole again by the election of a new man.

Peter's speech is interrupted by the account (1:18–19)
of the death of Judas. There is no point in trying to
harmonise the account with that in Mt 27:3–10. They
are both telling us that a wicked man met a violent death.
Matthew's description echoes (by the use of the same
verb) the death of the traitor, Achitophel, in 2 Sam 17:
23. He explains the title of the field as due to the fact that

it was bought with 'blood-money' (the blood of Jesus).
Luke's description, on the other hand, echoes the account
of the sinner 'falling headlong' in Wis 4 : 19. He explains
the title of the field as due to the fact that Judas' blood
was spilt there.

In the account of Matthias' election (1 : 26) it is possible that the 'casting of lots' is only metaphorical, high-
lighting the fact that he is God's choice, not man's (cf
Dupont, p 31, n 39).

*1. What are we to make of the 'necessity of fulfilling
the scriptures', so far as Judas' death is concerned?*

*2. Does the ordinary non-christian regard 'witnessing
to the resurrection' as a keynote of organised christianity?
If not, why not?*

Acts 2 : 1–13

We noticed earlier (1 : 6–11) the importance of considering the paschal mystery as a whole. The salvation-event
is only *complete* when the Son of Man, having broken
the bonds of death and sin, having been swept up into
the glory of God, has established, through the gift of the
Spirit, a *community* of 'new men' which is the beginning
of the eschatological rule of God in the fulfilled community of heaven.

Luke's account of the sending of the Spirit, packed
with old testament overtones, stresses this community
dimension. The group gathered 'together in one place'
are not the 'one hundred and twenty' of the preceding
verses, but the whole community of believers of 1 : 13–14.

The Jewish feast of Pentecost had its origins, as a harvest festival, in the Canaanite religions. As the feast of
unleavened bread became assimilated to the annual com-

memoration of the exodus from Egypt, so this 'feast of weeks', celebrated fifty days after the passover, became assimilated to the annual commemoration of the sealing of the covenant on Mount Sinai (cf Lev 23 : 15–16; Num 28 : 26; Ex 19 : 1–16). As the commemoration of the ancient salvation-event of the exodus had lasted fifty days (seven times seven plus one, denoting perfection and rest), so the sending of the Spirit on the fiftieth day 'seals' (cf Eph 1 : 13–14) the new salvation-event. Moreover, until chronology got the better of theology, the christian liturgy would celebrate the 'harvest' of redemption in the Spirit, of which Christ is the 'first-fruits' (1 Cor 15 : 20, 23; Rom 8 : 11; Col 1 : 18–20) as a *period* of fifty days, as the Jewish Pentecost had been the celebration of the harvest over a period of fifty days (cf Confraternity text of 2 : 1: 'And when the days of Pentecost were drawing to a close').

The imagery of wind and fire recall many earlier theophanies, or sensible manifestations of the divine power and presence, in particular that of Mount Sinai (cf Ex 19 : 16–20; 1 Kgs 19 : 11–12; Ps 104 : 29–32; Jn 3 : 6–8). Notice that Luke does not describe anything so banal as a mere 'appearance' of wind and flame: he is wrestling with the inexpressible ('a sound . . . *like* . . . wind'; 'tongues *as* of fire').

So far as the effect of the theophany is concerned, it seems probable that, as so often in the bible, two independent traditions have been merged. The first (2 : 4, 12 ff) would see the 'gift of tongues' as ecstatic (and therefore unintelligible) 'speaking with tongues', the sign of men completely 'taken over' by the Spirit (cf 1 Cor 14 : 1–25). The second (2 : 5–11) would see in the fact that the new community speaks in the accents of all men a sign that the destruction of human community through sin

(cf Gen 11 : 1–9) has been healed. Both ideas are important if we are to capture the full significance of Peter's
insistence, in the sermon he now preaches, that this
'coming of the Spirit' is the arrival of the eschatological
'day of the Lord'.

   *1. To what extent is the gift of the Spirit necessarily a
conscious experience?*
   *2. What useful purpose was (or is) served by 'ecstatic
utterance'?*

Acts 2:14–41 (also 3:12–26; 4:8–12; 5:29–32; 10:34–43; and 13:16–41)

In the course of Acts there are numerous discourses put
in the mouths of the principal characters. They differ
widely both in their purpose and in the audience to
whom they are directed. Thus we have Stephen's passion-
ate defence of Christ as the fulfilment of the old testament in Acts 7; Paul's somewhat unsuccessful attempt to
preach to the Athenians in Acts 17; Paul's farewell discourse to church leaders at Miletus in Acts 20; Paul's
account of his conversion before Agrippa in Acts 26; and
several others. But six of these discourses, or 'sermons',
stand out from all the rest and must be considered together. The preacher in five cases is Peter, and in the
remaining one Paul. In each case they are addressed to
unbelievers and aim at a message arousing the response
of faith: they are 'kerygma', or 'proclamation' of the
gospel message. Their fundamental importance lies not
so much in their antiquity (although they are among the
earliest elements of the new testament, reflecting the
earliest stage in the apostolic preaching) as in the fact that
they are condensed summaries of the whole apostolic

message, of the 'gospel of Jesus Christ'. They give us a synthesis of christian revelation in which the emphasis accorded to each element, and the interrelation of the elements, is as important as the content of each element considered in isolation.

In their content, and in their structure, they underlie the pattern of the canonical gospels. One could say that they stand in a similar relationship to the canonical gospels as does the 'capsule' account of the last supper at the centre of the great eucharistic prayer to the structure of the whole eucharistic liturgy. They remain normative, not only for all credal formulations of the christian faith, but also for the 'pattern' of even a highly developed dogmatic theology. In that sense in which it is true that the whole of revelation is 'contained' in the scriptures, it is also true that the whole of revelation is 'contained' in each of these discourses. Not that they include an adequate number of propositions for use as proof-texts with which to bombard one's theological adversaries, but that they form a *complete* statement of the identity and significance of Jesus Christ.

The church has constantly to be asking herself to what extent the *emphasis* in her presentation of revelation corresponds to this normative structure. The rediscovery, in our own day, of the unity and centrality of the paschal mystery in christian belief and liturgical practice, is an example of this process of self-questioning being successfully accomplished.

This pentecost sermon of Peter's is the first of these six sermons, the main elements of which are as follows (in the Appendix on pp 138–39 we have provided a comparative diagram, showing how these elements occur in each of the sermons):

A. Listen,
B. We are witnesses
C. that God has raised up
D. this Jesus whom you killed
E. (because you did not recognise his coming in word
   and work,
F. announced by the Baptist),
G. making him Lord and saviour;
H. in whose name all men are saved ('Jew first and
   then Greek'),
I. by the power of the Spirit,
J. that believe in him.
K. He it is who is the fulfilment of the scriptures, of
   God's mighty works,
   the Davidic messiah;
L. whose glorification introduces God's eschatological
   saving judgement.
M. Repent, believe, and be saved.

*1. If we were asked to give a summary of what our
christianity means to us, at what points would it differ
from the summary above?*
*2. How would 'repent . . . and be saved' translate into
language intelligible to the modern English unbeliever?*

Acts 2:42–47 (also 4:32–35 and 5:12–16)

The section on the life of the Jerusalem church (2 : 42–
5 : 42) includes three summary descriptions of the life of
the community (2 : 42–47; 4 : 32–35; 5 : 12–16). Each summary is followed by a narrative, giving a more detailed
account of events in the life of the church. Just as these
narratives have a didactic purpose, stressing the power
of the Spirit in the new people of God, and are far from

being bald 'accounts', so these summaries are idyllic, and somewhat stylised pictures of what the life of the church *ought* to be like.

The central theme is that of *fellowship* (2:42, 44–46; 4:32, 34–35; 5:12). The sharing of all things in common is an expression of the community's union of heart and mind. This life of fellowship is characterised by joy (2:46). The sources of fellowship are twofold: the teaching of the apostles (2:42; 4:33) and shared eucharistic worship (2:42, 46; cf 20:7; Lk 24:35; 1 Cor 10:16). It is important to stress the complete lack, in these accounts, of any divorce between word and sacrament, or between charismatic and hierarchical ministry. One also notices the power of the Spirit in the healing ministry of the apostles (2:43; 5:12, 15–16) and in the continual growth of the community (2:47; 5:14).

Finally, there is at this stage no break between the life of the new community and the patterns of religious expression of the people of the old covenant (2:46; 5:12).

1. To what extent are 'fellowship' and 'generosity' the keynotes of what goes on in our churches on a Sunday morning?

2. Is there any sense in which our work for some kind of economic parity in the world should be concerned firstly with the well-being of our fellow-christians?

3. How important is the frequent celebration of the Lord's supper for the health of a christian community?

Acts 3:1–4:35

The healing of the lame man by Peter is the occasion of the first clash with the Jewish authorities. Luke's care to show the *continuity* of the apostolic ministry with that of

Jesus (the wonder of the crowds, so reminiscent of Mark, the matter-of-fact way in which the church's persecution is linked to that of Jesus: 4 : 24–29) is only equalled by his concern to show the essential *differences*. When Jesus told a lame man to walk (cf Lk 5 : 20–25) he did so by his own power; when Peter does so (3 : 5–7) it is by the power ('in the name') of Jesus Christ of Nazareth (cf 4 : 30). In view of the close interrelationship between physical healing and spiritual healing (forgiveness) in the gospels, the implications of the apostles' ability to heal by the power of Jesus should not be overlooked.

The hallmark of Acts is the insistence that the entire work of the church is due to the presence of the Spirit; but to speak or act 'in the Spirit' is to speak or act 'in the name of Jesus' (notice how 4 : 8–12 recalls Mk 13 : 9–13).

The 'descent of the Spirit' at Pentecost is not a once-for-all event, but a continual dimension of the community's experience (cf 4 : 31 with 1 : 8; 2 : 1–4). The 'shaking' of the house again reminds us of the theophanies of the old testament (cf Ex 19 : 18; Ps 29). Just as the healing power of Jesus was not magical, but was correlative to the *receptivity* of those with whom he was dealing (cf Lk 5 : 20; Mk 6 : 5–6), so also the coming of the Spirit into the christian community is correlative to an attitude of receptivity ('And when they had prayed . . .'; cf 5 : 3, 9; 7 : 51).

1. Is faith-healing or scientific medical practice the more distinctively christian activity?

2. How are we to understand the impossibility of salvation except in the name of Jesus?

3. What is the place of private ownership in our understanding of human community?

Acts 4:36–5:16

The Ananias and Sapphira incident suggests that the complete sharing of possessions mentioned in the 'summaries' was voluntary, the criterion being the needs of the community (cf 2:45, 4:35). Peter's reproof (5:4) suggests that the couple's fault lay, not in failing to give all they had, but in *pretending* to have given everything over to the community. While the incident recalls that recounted in Josh 7 (cf Lev 27:28–29; the 'devoted things' of RSV is unhelpful: Confraternity's 'possessions which a man vows as doomed to the Lord' is clearer), there is one important difference. In Joshua, the whole community suffers the penalty for the sin of a few; in Acts, the stress on individual responsibility is more marked.

Are we right in finding the account of Ananias' and Sapphira's deaths a little indigestible?

Acts 5:17–32

It is not certain that the account of Peter's deliverance from prison (which may be another account of the escape described in Chapter 12) is necessarily intended to be understood as miraculous; it *is* certain that it is intended to be understood as due to the power of God, protecting his people and setting them free from their enemies (cf 5:19 with Mt 1:20; 2:19–20; Gen 16:7–14).

The high priest's charge (5:28) echoes the trial of Jesus in Matthew's account (cf Mt 27:25).

1. Is 'speaking out boldly' always the authentic christian reaction to opposition and hostility?
2. What is the relationship between apostolic witness and the witness of the Spirit, in the life of the church?

3. Is it an oversimplification to attribute, as Peter does, the resurrection *of Jesus to God, and his* death *to men?*

Acts 5:33–42

The attitude of Gamaliel reminds us of the dilemma with which our Lord confronted the Jewish authorities (cf Lk 20:1–8). The refusal of Gamaliel to 'take sides' is in interesting contrast to the mentality of his pupil, Paul (cf 22:3) who, at this time, was 'breathing threats and murder against the disciples of the Lord' (9:1). Is Gamaliel prudent or cowardly? Is Paul courageous or fanatical? Like the poor, these two mentalities are always with us.

The account of the church's life in Jerusalem in these early days is rounded off by another 'summary': in spite of, indeed *because of* (cf Mt 5:10–12), threats and persecutions, the community does not cease joyfully to preach the gospel.

To what extent is the survival and growth of the church a criterion of her authenticity?

3

The first missions
Acts 6:1–11:18

Acts 6:1–15

In the first two sections of Acts, the new people of God were seen in strict continuity with the old. Eschatological fulfilment, yes; newness of life in the Spirit; but still rooted in Jerusalem and worshipping in the temple. The cracking of the chrysalis can only happen slowly, and although the universality of the community was implicit in the Pentecost event, the tensions between the Jews from 'headquarters' and those from the diaspora provide the occasion for the first structural modifications to the community's way of life. Digging out the analogies between the evolution of the church in apostolic times and the implications of the second Vatican Council is a dangerous game, but it is not without interest that these tensions are the result of pastoral necessities on the periphery (6:1).

Although the word *diakonia* occurs several times in this narrative (cf 6:1), this is due to the fact that, throughout the new testament, it is a principal dimension of christian ministry. It is an anachronism to identify the 'seven' as 'deacons' (they are never referred to as such in the text). The threefold office of bishop, priest, and deacon is the result of a gradual process of crystallisation and clarification (it is significant that the Vatican Council, in its restoration of the diaconate, made no use of this section of Acts). In the same way, it would be anachronistic to ask: 'Does 6:6 refer to sacramental ordination?' Luke's primary purpose is to provide the background for the stories of Stephen and Philip. Nevertheless, it is interesting to notice that, while the 'commission to ministry' is performed by the apostles, with prayer and the imposition of hands (cf Num 27:16–18), it is only done after obtaining the consent of the community, which itself provided the candidates (6:5).

One notices again (cf 5:28) how the trial of Stephen echoes the trial of Jesus, and that the opposition to Stephen is identified with opposition to the Spirit of God (6:10; cf 5:3; 7:51).

1. Is the idea of 'worker-priests' a clerical invasion of distinctively lay (or diaconal!) activity?

2. To what extent should 'appointment to the ministry' be a democratic process?

Acts 7:1–54

The discourse put into the mouth of Stephen is intended to demonstrate that Jesus Christ is the fulfilment of the old testament but, in contrast with the six 'kerygmatic sermons', it is markedly polemical, laying continual emphasis on the blindness of Israel throughout her history. It contains nearly four dozen explicit quotations, mostly from Genesis and Exodus, and numerous implicit citations. That particular blindness that identifies 'true religion' with worship in any special *place* is excoriated towards the end but, although Isaiah (66:1–2) and Jeremiah (7:1–11) would have approved, christian theology has not yet developed to the point where Jesus himself (cf

Jn 2:19–22) and the members of his body (cf Eph 3:16) will be identified with the true dwelling-place of God in the Spirit.

1. Is not a loaded presentation of salvation-history, such as Stephen's discourse, a breeding-ground for anti-semitism?

2. Is the concept of a 'holy place' improper for chris-tianity?

Acts 7:55–8:3

The account of Stephen's death takes up where 6:15 left off, and now the comparison with the death of Jesus is even clearer. Christologically, the placing by Luke of Ps 31:6 in the mouths of the dying Jesus (cf Lk 23:46) and the dying Stephen (7:59), is very important, especially in view of the fact that Jesus hands his life over to the *Father*, whereas Stephen hands his life over to *Jesus*.

The section ends with the first mention of Saul (7:58; 8:1–3) and the beginning of the 'christian diaspora' (8:1).

What do we understand by 'standing at the right hand of God'?

Acts 8:4–13

With the mission of Philip to Samaria, the activity of the church is directed, for the first time, outside orthodox Jewry. The Samaritans, as 'heretical Jews', were also wait-ing for the messiah, and so Philip 'proclaimed to them the Christ' (8:5). One notices again the similarity be-tween the signs of healing performed by Philip (8:7) and those performed by the Lord himself.

What is the relationship between miracle and magic?

Acts 8:14–25

'Receiving the word of God' (8:14; cf 11:1) is a technical term in Acts for the faith that responds to the proclamation of the good news. The most difficult thing about this passage is to determine its precise significance for the later development of the rites of christian initiation. It would certainly be anachronistic to say: 'Here is the first account of the administration of the sacrament of confirmation', because the different *elements* in christian initiation (baptism, imposition of hands, first sharing in the eucharist) only became clearly distinct (but not separate) many years later. Nevertheless, the passage does provide evidence that, in the mind of the apostolic church, the incorporation of a believer into the community is incomplete until 'baptism in the name of the Lord Jesus' has been 'sealed' by the outpouring of the Spirit with a rite of imposition of hands performed by a delegate of the apostolic college.

1. Is it possible to distinguish, as this passage does, between 'reception of the word of God' and 'reception of the Spirit'?

2. What would Peter have made of the practice of giving mass-stipends?

Acts 8:26–40

The account of Philip's evangelising of the eunuch is interesting for a number of reasons. In the first place, it is another indication (cf 1:8) of the importance of the Isaian 'servant songs' for the christology of the apostolic church (8:32–33; cf Is 53:7–8).

Like so many passages in the new testament, it is strongly marked by the influence of the early baptismal liturgy; so strongly that an early commentator inserted an extract from the rite of baptism to highlight the eunuch's profession of faith (8 : 37, correctly relegated by most modern versions to a footnote).

Philip's dramatic disappearance is another reminder that every prophet (and every one who officially proclaims the word of God is a prophet) is acting as the agent of the Spirit of God (8 : 39, echoing 1 Kg 18 : 12; cf Ezek 3 : 12).

What makes a man a reliable guide to the interpretation of the scriptures?

Acts 9: 1–30

The conversion of Paul (it seems simpler to employ the Roman form of his name throughout, although Luke does not introduce it until 13 : 9) is one of the best-known and most dramatic incidents in Acts. It left so strong an impression on Paul himself that some scholars have even doubted whether his understanding of the christian mystery ever developed beyond the point reached in this initial encounter. Luke regards it as so important that he describes it three times (cf also 22 : 3–16; 26 : 9–18; Gal 1 : 11–17). As one would expect, the accounts differ in detail.

The first point to notice is that, once again, the theology of baptism has influenced the narrative. In the early church, 'illumination' was often a technical term for baptism; baptismal faith is a true 'seeing' of the Lord who is the way and the *truth*. In the second account, the blindness is explicitly stated to be due to 'too much light' (cf 22 : 11), and the more 'physical' account in this chapter

may be a later development of the narrative (cf Tb
11 : 10–15; Jn 9).

The calling of Paul is a *prophetic* vocation (9 : 15–cf
Jer 1 : 10; Ac 26 : 17—cf Jer 1 : 5–8; Is 42 : 7, 16). Again,
the Isaian servant songs are in the background, but applied this time not to the Lord himself, but to the man
chosen to share in the mystery of Christ.

The dramatic identification of the persecuted christians with their risen Lord (9 : 4–5; 22 : 8–9; 26 : 14–15)
recalls the similar identification made in Jesus' description of the last judgement (cf Mt 25 : 31–46). This
conviction that the risen Lord is encountered in the
members of his mystical body, the church, will remain
central to Paul's thought, finding its fullest expression in
the 'captivity epistles'.

It is important to notice that, in Paul's mind, this first
encounter with the risen Christ is as real as the resurrection appearances to the other apostles recorded in the
gospels (cf 1 Cor 15 : 3–8). This highlights the point we
made earlier (cf notes on 1 : 6–11) that it is the *death* of
the Lord that is his 'going away', rather than his glorification (ascension) at the right hand of the Father, which
makes possible his fuller presence to his followers in the
gift of the Spirit.

*1. Is all oppressive denial of human rights and liberties
a 'persecution of the Lord' or only the formal persecution
of a christian for his beliefs?*

*2. Paul seems to have been dramatically assisted in the
discovery of his vocation: what 'signs' would most of us
expect?*

Acts 9:31–10:43

After another 'summary' of the life of the community
(9 : 31), Peter's activity outside the area of Judea and
Samaria prepares the ground for the account of the conversion of Cornelius.

The conversion of Cornelius is, in Luke's plan, an
event of immense significance. It represents the most
radical breakthrough in that universalising of the gospel
which is the central theme of Acts. The Jewish religion
had always admitted non-Jews to membership, but on
condition that they *became* Jews, culturally as well as
spiritually, through circumcision and the adoption of the
practices enjoined by the law. The greatest problem
faced by the apostolic church was: granted that the gospel
is to be preached to 'every nation', to what extent does
faith in Christ demand acceptance of the cultural and religious traditions of the old people of God? The case of
Cornelius occasions the beginnings of an understanding
of the answer, which will find a fuller formulation in the
Council of Jerusalem (cf 15 : 1–35).

Cornelius is described as 'a just man who feared God'
(10 : 2). This is a technical term to denote that he was a
follower of the Jewish religion, probably attending the
synagogue, without having been fully integrated through
circumcision (cf 10 : 22, 35; 13 : 16, 26).

The regulations governing ritual purity and impurity
in matters of food were complex in judaism, as in any
primitive religion (cf Lev 11). Some prohibitions were
directly religious, such as those concerned with food
offered to pagan idols: these will continue to present a
problem for the christian conscience (cf 1 Cor 9; Rom
14). Peter's revulsion at the command to eat such forbidden food is hardly surprising; but the voice is quite
uncompromising: 'What God has cleansed, do not thou

call common' (10:15). The christian community has not
always been as prompt in assimilating this message as
Peter was.

*If it is universally true that we should 'not call any
man common or unclean', what place is there for social
controls to protect the 'faith of the weak' from contamina-
tion?*

Acts 10:44–11:18

Luke insists on the parallel between the 'pagans' Pentecost' which now takes place, and the original event in the
upper room (notice the gift of tongues, 10:46; cf also
11:15). Naturally 'the believers from among the circum-
cised . . . were amazed' (10:45) to realise that the messianic
outpouring of the Spirit affects not only orthodox Jews
(2:4) and schismatic Samaritans (8:17), but also these
pagans. It is clear from the criticism Peter meets in Jerusalem (11:2) that the real bone of contention is not that
these men should have been baptised, but that they
should have been accepted while remaining uncircum-
cised, and therefore outside the Jewish community. The
shock the Jews receive is comparable to the shock that an
orthodox christian would receive at seeing an unbaptised
man admitted to the eucharist; a shock that would not
imply bigotry on the part of the christian, nor a refusal
to admit the working of the Spirit outside the church.

The sacramental theologian need not lose too much
sleep over the fact that, on this unique occasion, the outpouring of the Spirit took place *before* baptism (10:44–
48). What is unusual is the 'full' gift of the Spirit, not
any activity of the Spirit in the heart of the catechumen.
After all, according to the normal pattern of christian

initiation, baptismal incorporation into the community makes permanent, and gives visible expression to, the salvation-situation of one who has been given the gift (in the Spirit) of christian faith.

What principles should govern common worship between christians and non-christian theists?

4

Antioch: the new centre
Acts 11:19–14:27

Acts 11:19–30

According to one ancient tradition, supported by a
variant reading of 11:28, Luke himself was a member of
the original christian community at Antioch. Whether or
not this is the case, he certainly shows a great interest in
the church at Antioch. Up to this point, although he has
described missionary activity in Samaria, Caesarea, and
elsewhere, the only *centre* of christian life has been Jerusalem. Now, for the first time, there is described another
centre of missionary activity, another church, anxious to
keep in communion with the mother-church at Jerusalem.

The narrative takes up where it left off at 8:4, and
links the foundation of the church at Antioch with the
dispersal that followed the death of Stephen. The 'for-
eigners' who evangelise 'the Greeks' preach not 'Jesus the
Christ' (the messianic title would have been unintelligible to a non-Jewish audience), but 'the *Lord* Jesus'
(11:20; the *kyrios*, the divine Lord of history).

Barnabas goes to Tarsus, Paul's home town, to enlist
him as a fellow-missionary (11:25; cf 9:30; Gal 1:21).
It is difficult to be certain about the dating of Paul's
movements, but it seems likely that, after his conversion

and 'retreat' in the desert (cf Gal 1:17; 2 Cor 11:32), he returned to Tarsus to await further orders.

The fact that 'in Antioch the disciples were for the first time called christians' (11:26) indicates that the church is now recognised as a religious group distinct both from judaism and from paganism.

In the lists of 'spiritual gifts', that of 'prophet' (11:27) is usually placed second after that of 'apostle' (cf 1 Cor 12:28–29; Eph 4:11). While it is true that, particularly in Paul's usage, the various gifts within the community cannot be placed into tidy categories, nevertheless the difference between the 'prophet' and the 'teacher' (cf 13:1) is that the former is called to interpret the present moment in terms of the words and deeds of salvation-history, whereas the latter's function is to ensure the systematic teaching within the community. It is not too inaccurate to say that, in modern terminology, the 'teacher' is the preacher or catechist, whereas the 'prophet' is the theologian (and the implication of 'proclamation' in the prophetic vocation underlines the fact that he, too, is concerned with kerygma, with announcing the gospel).

The Vatican Council has awakened in all the churches of the Roman catholic communion their responsibility to assist each other, materially as well as spiritually. Dr Cullmann had already suggested that 'ecumenical collections' are a practical way of awakening and expressing ecumenical concern. The idea has a long history (11:29), and it was a favourite with Paul (cf 24:17; 1 Cor 16:1; 2 Cor 8:3–4; 9:6–15; Rom 15:25–32).

1. If the principal function of a bishop is to preach, what should be the role of the theologian in the church?

2. What should be the place of ecclesiastically organised economic activity and assistance in the modern world?

Acts 12:1–24

This account of Peter's trial and escape from prison (which may be another version of that described in 5:17–28) fits somewhat uneasily into its context, and the rather vague 'about that time' (12:1) reminds us of the frequently artificial chronology of the gospels.

Can we meaningfully regard personal disaster as 'divine judgement'?

Acts 12:25–14:27

Paul's missionary career, as recounted in Acts, is usually divided into three 'journeys' (13:1–14:27; 15:36–18:22; 18:23–20:38). In fact, this division is artificial and misleading. Paul had no 'headquarters'; during the period in question (c AD 45–58) he was usually on the move, but sometimes spent long periods in one place (over two years, for example, at Ephesus: 55–57). We shall, however, refer to the 'three journeys' in these notes, to facilitate the use of standard works on Paul's missionary activity.

Paul and Barnabas are not self-appointed missionaries. They are delegated by the community (13:3), acting in obedience to the Holy Spirit (13:2), who guides the journey (13:4) and inspires their preaching (13:9).

To preach to 'Jew first, then Greek' (cf Rom 1:16) is a general principle of Paul's: it is only *within* the christian community that this distinction has been abolished (cf Rom 10:12–13). This is why, on arriving in a town, he usually goes first to the synagogue, and begins to proclaim the gospel in the context of the customary 'sharing of witness' that takes place after the reading of the scriptures (cf 13:5, 15; 14:1; 17:10, etc).

The rest of this section describes the mounting opposition to Paul's preaching: something he is never likely to forget (cf 2 Cor 11:25; 2 Tim 3:11). The source of this opposition is, at this stage, those Jews who refuse the gospel message (14:2); later it will be the Jewish converts to christianity who found the implications of the decision of the Council of Jerusalem hard to swallow (this is the common interpretation of the 'judaisers' who plagued Paul's life: cf 2 Cor 11–12; Gal 1–4. However, as on most interesting questions, 'the experts are divided'). Luke has been charged with being responsible for the first stirrings of anti-semitism in christianity. The charge loses some of its force if we bear in mind that, for Luke, as for John, 'the Jews' refers to those members of the chosen people who reject, in whatever measure, Christ and the liberty he came to bring, and do so on the basis of the Mosaic law. It must be admitted, however, that Luke makes no attempt to give us an unbiased account of Paul's missionary activity. In the second half of Acts he is passionately concerned to defend Paul against his critics, and the result, inevitably, is that we are seeing these events from a particular, limited point of view.

1. Does the fact that a modern account of missionary activity would probably give less prominence to the Spirit, necessarily mean that we underestimate the primacy of the Spirit in the growth of the church?

2. How is the christian preacher to decide which elements in a pre-christian culture are 'vain things' (14:15)?

5
The council of Jerusalem
Acts 15:1–35

The critical incident with which this chapter is concerned probably took place in AD 49. It is difficult to relate it with certainty to the various other trips to and from Jerusalem mentioned in Acts and Galatians, but it seems likely that 11 : 27–30 refers to the same events, and that Luke mentioned them there to round off his narrative at that point.

The text of this chapter raises a number of problems. Whether Paul and Barnabas had come up to hand over money collected for the community in Judea (11 : 30) or to protest against judaising activities in Antioch (15 : 1–2), or both, it is strange that, on arrival, they seem to have forgotten what they came about (15 : 4). Even more curious is the fact that, ten years later, James seems to find it necessary to inform Paul (21 : 25) of the decision of a meeting at which they had both been present!

A great deal of ink has been spilt in discussing the question as to whether James' 'judgement' (15 : 19) impugns the primacy of Peter. In view of the fact that a clear understanding of the pattern of relationships within the order of christian ministry only developed slowly, the discussion appears a little unreal. James, at this period, is the leader of the mother-church at Jerusalem (cf 12 : 17; 21 : 18; Gal 2 : 9), and therefore a key figure in the debate. Moreover, Peter's contribution to the debate seems perfectly consistent with the essential role of the primate as the 'fundamental principle of unity of faith and communion' (Vatican II, *Constitution on the Church*, art 18).

The problem that faced the council of Jerusalem is one with which the church is permanently confronted. To what extent does the christian life, a life of faith in the risen Christ, the 'universal man', involve the adoption of particular cultural forms within which the gospel has, historically, found expression? There is no tidy answer to this question.

To affirm that *every* context within which the word of God has been mediated to men remains permanently and exclusively valid and binding on those who respond to that word in faith, is not only to impose a particular, limited expression of the word, thus frustrating its *universal* intelligibility and applicability, it is also formally to deny the essential nature of salvation as an *historical process*.

To affirm, on the other hand, that earlier cultural settings of the 'gospel tradition' are *irrelevant* to a later age is to overlook the fact that the transcendent word of God is only communicated to us in particular words and events which, *as* the historical communication of the word to men, retain a permanent validity and relevance.

In other words, both approaches undermine the paradox of the incarnation. The first involves an implicit denial of the universality of the word, proclaimed to *all* men, in *all* situations. The second involves an implicit denial of the concrete, historical process within which the word is spoken to us. The first reduces christianity to a history without contemporary significance, the second reduces it to a 'significance' without objective historical embodiment.

The council of Jerusalem achieved a fundamental breakthrough with its realisation that the law of Moses was only relevant as a *preparation* for Jesus Christ (cf 15 : 11). Like any radical development in the church's self-understanding, it was due to the activity of the Holy Spirit guiding the church into all truth (15 : 28), its full implications were not immediately evident (as the letters of Paul and the remainder of Acts will demonstrate), its initial formulation was imperfect and hedged with compromise (15 : 28–29).

The problem remains. It is the principal problem in interpreting the scriptures (is the eucharist a permanent feature in the life of the church, is the petrine office permanent, is the covering of women's heads in church a distinctive feature of christian life from Calvary to the second coming?). It is the central problem that faced the second Vatican Council (is the Latin liturgy an indispensable element in the life of the Western church, is the philosophical language of Greece, Rome, and medieval Europe a perennially privileged vehicle of theological discourse, is the ordination of women to the priesthood permanently excluded because it has never happened?). In many respects, the decrees of Vatican II show the same characteristics as that of the council of Jerusalem: a fundamental breakthrough whose implications are not immediately evident, and the initial formulation of which is imperfect and hedged with compromise.

A parallel was suggested, in the notes, between Jerusalem and Vatican II. Perhaps the discussion could be developed in relation to specific points found in the council's decrees?

6

Paul's second and third journeys
Acts 15:36–20:38

Acts 15:36–17:14

The Council of Jerusalem marks the principal division
in the structure of Acts. From now on, as a result of the
decision taken there, the mission to the gentiles, and
therefore Paul, the apostle to the gentiles (cf Gal 2:8),
are at the centre of the picture. Although there are no
new major doctrinal themes to be stated, this does not
mean that the account of Paul's activity is 'mere narrative'. The goal of his mission is the 'universalising' of the
gospel (cf notes on 1:1–5), and the familiar refrains about
the growth of the community (16:5) and the missionary's
guidance by the Spirit (16:6–7) continue to appear.

Timothy, as the son of a christian Jewess and a gentile
(16:1), is in a situation not directly envisaged by the
Council of Jerusalem. Paul circumcises him to avoid
scandalising the Jewish christians unnecessarily (16:3).

16:10–17 is, with the possible exception of 11:28, the
first of the 'we-sections'. The use of the first person plural
in these passages has given rise to considerable discussion,
but it is fairly certain that, whether or not Luke is using
a written source, he intends to indicate that he was himself one of Paul's travelling companions.

The baptism of Lydia, 'with her household' (16:15),
is the first of three similar cases in Acts (cf 16:29–34;

18:8) that are of great importance for the theology of baptism. The 'household' almost certainly refers, not only to the adult members of the family and to slaves, but also to the children, if any. In view of the constant stress in the new testament on the necessity of saving faith as a precondition of baptism, it is of considerable significance that only the 'heads' of the families appear to have been questioned about their faith. Whether or not the other adults were so questioned, the real importance of these passages lies in the fact that they almost certainly provide evidence for infant baptism in the time of St Paul. And, if this is the case, it does not mean that faith was regarded as unimportant in the case of infants, but that they were received into the community in virtue of the faith of their *parents*. It seems certain that infant baptism was not the *invariable* custom of the early church: but, in cases when it was omitted, this was not due to any lack of interest in the salvation of the infant, but in virtue of the *same principle*: the faith of the parents.

1. In what circumstances should infant baptism normally be refused?

2. From what points of view is the instinct of some christian parents, that the children should 'be left to decide for themselves', a sound one?

Acts 17:15–18:22

Luke's suggestion (17:15) that Timothy remained behind in Thessalonica seems to be an oversimplification in the interests of clarity. According to 1 Thess 3:1–6, Timothy accompanied Paul to Athens, was sent back by him to Thessalonica, and later rejoined him at Corinth.

Paul's discourse to the Areopagus (the term may refer

to the Hill of Mars but, more probably, to the city council, which formerly used to meet there) is unique in Acts.
Faced with a sophisticated Greek audience, he does not
base his preaching on the history of salvation, but on the
knowledge of God attainable without revelation (cf Rom
1:19–25; Eph 4:17–19). He does not use the themes and
images of scripture, but of Greek philosophy and poetry
(17:28–29). He has difficulty in showing how the raising
to life of 'the man whom (God) has appointed' (17:31)
fits into this picture, the audience is unimpressed (17:
32), and Paul abandons the technique (cf 1 Cor 1:17–
25). In our own day, however, the problem has arisen
with particular urgency: how is Christ to be preached to
people wholly unfamiliar with the world of the bible?

Paul moves to Corinth, where he stays for eighteen
months, then returns to Antioch by way of Ephesus (18:
19) and (possibly) Jerusalem (18:22).

1. Would it be fair to describe Honest to God *as 'a
modern discourse to the Areopagus'?*

*2. Apart from this one occasion, there is little evidence
that Paul regarded pagan culture with any respect. How
is a keen awareness of the exhaustive validity of christian
revelation to be integrated with a sensitive respect for the
values of contemporary atheism?*

Acts 18:23–19:7

Before describing Paul's return to Ephesus, Luke mentions Apollos for the first time. The latter's eloquence
and dynamism later made him a centre of controversy
(cf 1 Cor 1:12; 3:4–23); according to one ancient tradition, he wrote the letter to the Hebrews. He is further
catechised by Priscilla and Aquila, who had met Paul in

Corinth (cf 18:2) and were later to return to Rome (cf Rom 16:3; 1 Cor 16:19). As with the twelve others Paul encounters at Ephesus, Apollos 'knew only the baptism of John' (18:25; 19:1–7). Their ignorance of the Holy Spirit (19:2) seems to have been an ignorance, in particular, of the Spirit's role in animating the messianic community. The imposition of hands by the apostle, following their baptism, is the occasion of another 'Pentecost' (19:5–6; cf 8:14–17).

How could Apollos have 'spoken and taught accurately the things concerning Jesus', if he 'knew only the baptism of John'?

Acts 19:8–20:16

Luke tells us little about the two (three? cf 20:31) years in Ephesus, but 19:12 would appear to provide the first evidence of the use of relics in the church. The account of the mission at Ephesus closes, appropriately, with a 'growth refrain' (19:20).

The account of the silversmiths' riot has been fitted in here rather untidily by Luke, after he has announced Paul's decision to return to Greece (19:21). The mention of Rome at this point (19:21) is a device by Luke to keep the plan of the book in the reader's mind.

The focal point of the cult of Artemis, or Diana, at Ephesus was the huge temple of the fertility goddess, containing her statue. The sale of silver models of the temple and statue was not helped by the success of Paul's preaching. There is little evidence in Luke's account that he considers the motives of the rioters to have been basically religious.

The second 'we-section' began at 20:5 and continues

as far as Paul's arrival at Jerusalem (cf 21:18); the insertion of the Miletus discourse somewhat obscures the unity of this section.

At Troas, Paul preaches during the celebration of the eucharist 'on the first day of the week' (20:7): the Lord's day (cf 1 Cor 16:2; Mt 28:1). It is good to discover that another old christian tradition, that of boring the congregation to death, dates back to apostolic times.

The 'day of Pentecost' which Paul is hurrying back to Jerusalem to celebrate (20:16) is, of course, the Jewish feast (cf notes on 2:1–3). The early church knew only one feast, that of Easter, the Lord's day, celebrated weekly. When an annual feast of Easter was introduced (and was known as 'the great Lord's day') it was celebrated over a period of fifty days. But the idea of having a feast to mark each *element* in the paschal mystery (death, resurrection, glorification, outpouring of the Spirit) did not develop until much later (fourth century), when the *unity* of the paschal mystery had begun to lose its grip on the christian consciousness (cf notes on 1:6–11).

What place has the use of relics in 'religion pure and undefiled'?

Acts 20:17–38

Paul's farewell address to the elders at Miletus is pastoral rather than doctrinal in content. He offers, without arrogance, the witness of his own ministry as an example of the 'pastoral style' that should characterise the christian minister. Luke highlights the fact that this is Paul's 'pastoral last will and testament' (cf 20:25, 36–38); from his arrest in Jerusalem until Acts ends in Rome, Paul will not again be seen as a free agent. If the pastoral epistles (the letters to Timothy and Titus) have Paul for their author, which is open to doubt, then there is ample evidence that he did in fact visit the churches of Asia Minor again (cf 1 Tim 1:3; 4:13; Tit 3:12; 2 Tim 4:13, 20). But these later journeys (between the years 58 and 67) are outside the scope of Acts.

The fact that the 'elders' are referred to both as *presbyteroi* (20:17) and *episkopoi* (20:28) is a reminder that to search for a distinction between 'bishops' and 'priests' at this period is fruitless (cf notes on 6:1–7).

In his letters, Paul makes remarkably little use of explicit quotations from the teaching of Christ. It is interesting to notice that, on one of the rare occasions he does so (20:35), he quotes a maxim not recorded in the canonical gospels.

What activities that we feel entitled to expect of the modern christian minister are not mentioned in Paul's apologia?

7

Paul, a prisoner for Christ
Acts 21:1–28:31

Acts 21:1–26

The journey from Miletus to Jerusalem is an excellent
illustration of Luke's use of geography to make theological statements. To grasp the full significance of the narrative, we have to compare his handling of the same
theme in his gospel.

The gospel begins in the temple of Jerusalem, the
heart and centre of the old covenant, and the infancy
narrative culminates in the finding of the child Jesus in
'his Father's house' (cf Lk 2:46–49).

The central section of the gospel is, like this chapter
of Acts, set in the form of a journey up to Jerusalem. The
irrevocable decision announced at Lk 9:51 corresponds
to Acts 20:22–23 (cf 19:21). Once the decision has been
taken, the narrative is punctuated by reminders of the
goal (Lk 10:38; 13:22, 33; 17:11; 18:31; 19:28; cf Acts
21:4–5, 12–15), and that goal is not simply Jerusalem,
but the suffering and death that awaits Jesus (and Paul:
the fact that he died in Rome does not detract from the
significance of his *arrest* in Jerusalem: Lk 9:22, 44; 12:
49–50; 18:31–33; cf Acts 20:22–24; 21:4, 11–13). Paul,
like Jesus, is wholly concerned with doing the will of
God (21:14; cf Lk 22:42). Finally, the last scenes are
played out where the drama began: in the temple itself,

149

the obsolescent symbol of God's covenant with his people
(21:26; cf Lk 2:46–49; 19:45–21:37; 23:44–46; 24:
49–53). It is clear from the accusations brought against
Paul (21:20–21), and from his letters (especially Romans), that he had gone beyond the explicit provisions
of the Council of Jerusalem, and had come to see that
the ground of justification for *all* men (Jew and gentile)
was saving faith in Jesus Christ, and not the works of the
old law. On the other hand, as we saw in the case of
Timothy (cf notes on 15:36–16:9), he did not discourage
the Jewish converts from continuing to observe the pre-
scriptions of the Mosaic law (cf 1 Cor 7:17–20). This is
now shown again by his assistance of the four men bound
by the Nazarite vow (21:23–26; cf Num 6:13–21). But
when passions are enflamed, logical conduct carries little
weight, and Paul's fate is sealed.

*Do we find it odd that Luke should have conveyed
theological meaning in a geographical narrative? What
other language could he have used to put across this kind
of theological meaning?*

Acts 21:27–40
In the account of the arrest, against the background of
the mob, there are once again echoes of the trial of Jesus.
Paul, like Jesus, is accused of preaching against the
temple (21:28; cf Mt 26:61). Jesus had been tried in
conjunction with the brigand Barabbas (Lk 23:18–19):
Paul is mistaken for the Egyptian who 'recently stirred
up a revolt' (21:38).

*What would stop us describing the arrest and trial of a
contemporary christian (Dietrich Bonhoeffer, say, or*

Albert Luthuli) in terms of the arrest and trial of Jesus?
A modern concern for historical accuracy? A suspicion
that it would be 'blasphemous'? Or something else?

Acts 22:1–26:32

These chapters include three 'apologias' by Paul: one
before the Jewish crowd, one before the Roman pro-
curator (24 : 10–21) and one before King Agrippa (26 : 1–
23). The first and third of these include further accounts
of Paul's conversion (cf notes on 9 : 1–30). On this occasion, Paul is at pains to stress his orthodox Jewish background, but any hope of pacifying the crowd is removed
by his final cry: 'I will send you far away to the gentiles'
(21 : 21). Jesus had warned his follower that 'they will lay
their hands on you . . . delivering you up to the syna-
gogues . . . kings and governors' (Lk 21 : 12). Accordingly,
after his arrest, Paul appears before the Sanhedrin (23),
Felix the governor (24), and King Agrippa (25–26).

Before the sanhedrin, Paul tries to drive a wedge between the pharisees and the sadducees, claiming that, like
any pharisee, he has only been concerned with 'the resurrection of the dead' (23 : 6; cf 24 : 14–15; Mt 22 : 23). To
the modern christian, for whom the resurrection of the
dead tends to mean very little (in spite of the creed),
Paul's argument seems dishonest, because the pharisees
certainly did *not* accept the fact of the resurrection of our
Lord. But we must remember that, for Paul, the resurrection of Christ as the pledge of *our* resurrection was a
central theme in his preaching (cf Rom 5–6; 1 Cor 15;
Col 1 : 18; 1 Thes 4 : 13–17).

Now that Luke has made his point about the significance of *Jerusalem* as the place of Paul's arrest, he can
begin to stress again, in the overall pattern of his book,

the significance of *Rome* (22 : 25–28; 23 : 11; 25 : 8–12; 26 : 32).

Maintaining the similarities between these years of imprisonment (24 : 27) and the trial of Jesus, there is a marked similarity between the relationship of Festus to Agrippa and that of Pilate to Herod. Like Jesus, Paul is innocent (23 : 29; 25 : 18; 26 : 31; cf Lk 23 : 14–15, 22) but, by his appeal to the imperial court, he has placed himself outside Festus' jurisdiction.

1. Why does the resurrection of the dead mean so little for the modern christian? How could it mean more?

2. Does Luke's emphasis of Paul's innocence intend only to relate Paul to Jesus, or does it intend too to inform christians that they must expect to suffer for their faith unjustly?

3. How far is the christian justified in claiming advantages on the basis of membership of a privileged group in society (cf 22 :25)?

Acts 27:1–28:16
Luke, who had accompanied Paul to Jerusalem, also travels with him to Rome (cf notes on 16 : 10–17 : 14; 20 : 7–16), but the graphically detailed account of the journey should not let us overlook the parallel that Luke draws between the storm off Crete and the journey of Jonah (27 : 9–44; cf Jon 1 : 4–16).

Paul's shipwreck is assimilated to the story of Jonah and his storm at sea. What does Luke mean by this paralleling? And what does it mean for us?

Acts 28:17–31

With the arrival of Paul in Rome his mission is complete. These verses summarise his career. Preaching first to Jew (28 : 23) then to 'Greek' (28 : 28), he proclaims the coming of the kingdom, the fulfilment of the law, in the person of Jesus (28 : 23, 31). As throughout the history of salvation (28 : 25–27), too many of those who are called refuse the invitation (but the warning is as relevant to the new people of God as the old).

The refusal of individuals, however, cannot ultimately frustrate the work of the Spirit. Luke has completed his task of compiling 'a narrative of the things which have been accomplished amongst us' (Lk 1 : 1); he has shown the church, growing in the power of the Spirit, witnessing to the risen Lord 'to the ends of the earth' (1 : 8), and leaves us with the picture of Paul, in Rome, the centre of the world, 'preaching the kingdom of God and teaching about the Lord Jesus quite openly and unhindered' (28 : 31).

'Some were convinced by what he said, while others disbelieved' (28 : 24)—so, in a nutshell, the story of all preaching of the gospel in all ages. Should we expect one day to succeed in convincing everyone?

Appendix: the structure of six sermons (cf p. 106)

Notice how even the shortest of the sermons contains all the essential elements. The old testament overtones in each case are of course much richer than the explicit quotations noted in the table would suggest.

	Acts 2:14–39 Occasion: outpouring of Spirit at pentecost	Acts 3:12–26 Occasion: healing of lame man	Acts 4:8–12 Occasion: healing of lame man	Acts 5:29–32 Occasion: trial by sanhedrin	Acts 10:34–43 Occasion: conversion of Cornelius	Acts 13:16–41 Occasion: Paul in synagogue at Pisidian Antioch
A	2:14 2:22		4:10			13:16 13:26
B	2:32	3:15		5:32	10:39 10:41	13:31
C	2:24 2:32	3:15 3:26	4:10	5:30	10:40	13:30
D	2:23 2:36	3:13–15	4:10	5:30	10:39	13:28
E	2:22	3:17			10:36–38	13:27
F					10:37	13:24
G	2:33 2:36	3:20	4:10	5:31	10:36	13:23

H	2:21 2:39	3:16	4:10 4:12	5:31	10:35 10:43	13:38–39
I	2:33			5:32	10:38	13:39
J	2:38	3:16	4:12	5:32	10:43	13:39
K	2:16–21 (cf Joel 3:1–5) 2:25–31 (cf Ps 15:8–11) 2:34–35 (cf Ps 109:1)	3:18 3:22–24 (cf Dt 18:15, 19 and Lv 25:29) 3:13	4:11 (cf Ps 117:22)	5:30	10:43	13:27 13:29 13:32–37 (cf Ps 2:7; Ps 55:3; Ps 15:10) 13:17–23
L	2:16–20	3:20–21	4:12	implied by 5:31	10:42	13:29
M	2:38	3:26	4:12	5:32	10:43	13:38–39

1 Peter

Bernard Robinson

Introduction

The authorship and structure of 1 Peter

The authorship, date, and structure of 1 Peter have for the last half-century been very much a bone of contention, and it cannot be said that any point of view has yet gained anything like general acceptance among scholars. As these differences of view do affect one's understanding of the work at some points, it will be well to give a brief summary of the history and present state of the controversies.

The disagreements concern principally the nature of the section 1:3–4:11. Is this central section, as it ostensibly appears, part of an apostolic letter, or is it (*a*) a baptismal homily, or (*b*) a baptismal liturgy, worked up, through the editorial addition of 1:1–2 and 4:12–5:14, into the form of an epistle?

The first suggestion that 1 Peter was a disguised baptismal homily was made in 1911 by R. Perdelwitz, and independently in 1919 by W. Bornemann, and numerous scholars have since adopted this view. The idea may, on the surface, seem very implausible, but there are quite strong arguments in its favour. There does seem to be a definite break at 4:11, which, with its solemn doxology, sounds very much like the end of a work ('. . . that God may universally be praised in Jesus Christ, to whom is the glory and the power for age upon age, Amen'), and the words standing at the end of 1 Peter—'I have written to you briefly', 1 Pet 5 : 12—are more apt if they refer to 4 : 12 ff. as a separate entity than if they refer to the whole document. Now if the two halves of 1 Peter were indeed originally separate, the case for the first half not having been originally written as a letter becomes quite strong. But why a baptismal homily (i.e., a sermon on baptism, delivered most plausibly at an actual baptismal service)? In the first place, the constant reference to baptismal themes, e.g., to begetting-anew and rebirth (1 : 3; 1 : 23; 2 : 2 etc.), to light (2 : 9—a common image of baptism in the early church), and in one case explicitly to baptism (3 : 21), indicate a strong baptismal preoccupation in the work; in the second place, we may point to the frequent occurrence in the text of Greek words for 'now', which may indicate a rite in actual progress—e.g., 'the things which have *now* been announced to you' (1 : 12), '*now* you are God's people' (2 : 10), 'you are *now* returned to the Shepherd and Guardian of your souls' (2 : 25), '. . . baptism *now* saves you' (3 : 21); also it may be argued that the expression 'like newborn babes' (2 : 2) is strictly applicable only to the recently baptised.

Those who regard the work as a liturgy rather than a homily tend to divide the section up, putting some of the words in the mouth of the presiding bishop, or presbyter, others in the mouths of the baptisands and others, instead of taking the whole section as an address by the bishop.

It is not possible in such a brief introduction to do justice to the arguments used on behalf of the homily/liturgy theories, but if the reader will take the trouble to read 1 : 3–4 : 11 to himself and try to see the passage as an early-church version of the paschal-vigil service he may, like the present writer, find that this imparts fresh meaning to the section; he may also find himself interested enough to investigate the matter further. For myself, I do not say I am convinced of the case, but I do find it very suggestive.

In any case, it is hazardous to make *too* strict a division between the two parts of 1 Peter. T. G. C. Thornton (*Journal of Theological Studies* xii, 1 April 1961) has shown that the two parts not only have a unity of theological outlook but also several words which occur in both parts are to be found nowhere else in the new testament. Thus it seems likely that the same man must have written both (although perhaps at different times), or he must have edited the first and written the second part.

It is possible to maintain that 1 Peter is a baptismal homily/liturgy and still accept the petrine authorship, though this is unusual among scholars. On the other hand, even if one rejects the homily/liturgy hypothesis it by no means follows that one must accept the petrine authorship. For my part, I am quite sure that the apostle Peter was not—in the usual sense of the word—the author of 1 Peter, although his name is attached to it (this presents no difficulty: there are abundant instances in the old testament and in the Jewish intertestamental literature of anonymous authors attaching, without any apparent intention of deceit, famous names to their own work—eg Solomon, in the case of Proverbs, the Song of Songs, and Wisdom). The fact is that the Greek style of the work is much too elegant and correct for a Galilean fisherman: the Greek of 1 Peter is much better than that of St Paul, and it is quite inconceivable that Peter, even if he could write Greek (or indeed write at all—in Acts 4:13 Luke describes him as 'uneducated, common'), could have written better Greek than the educated Paul, in fact the best Greek in the new testament after that of Hebrews.

Other arguments urged against the petrine authorship seem to me more precarious—for instance, the argument that the second half of 1 Peter (if not the first) presupposes a period of official state persecution such as did not occur until the time of Trajan (AD 98–117), and that the echoes of the epistles of Paul which we catch throughout 1 Peter indicate that the author knew the pauline epistles in a collected form, which would probably not be possible before about the end of the first century. In reply to the first point, it has been plausibly answered that there is nothing in 1 Peter to prove that the persecutions in question, however grievous, were official and actuated by the government, rather than the spasmodic police interventions by which the church was threatened from the earliest times; and as for similarities with St Paul, it seems to me that more work has to be done on this subject before we can be sure that the explanation is not, as Boismard for instance maintains, that in the phrases common to 1 Peter and Paul both were quoting hymns and credal formulas already in existence.

In 1 Pet 5:12 the author says 'I have written to you . . . by Silvanus', and it has been argued that this means that the actual writing of the epistle was done by Silvanus. By this argument it is possible to maintain an indirect authorship for St Peter, who will be supposed to have provided Silvanus with the general ideas of the epistle and left it to him to write them up. This hypothesis loses some of its probability when we remember that Silvanus had a hand in the composition of the Thessalonian letters (see 1 Thess 1:1; 2 Thess 1:1), for it is difficult to find much in common between 1 Peter and the Thessalonian letters.

We must therefore leave the disputes over authorship, date, and structure unresolved. 1 Peter may, or may not, be two epistles lumped together; may, or may not, be a homily/liturgy plus a letter; may, or may not, have the hand (but definitely not the pen, in my opinion) of Peter behind it. One need not take sides on these questions, but as one reads 1 Peter it is as well to have all the possibilities in mind.

Finally, a brief word about the general gist of the book. Throughout, the author is very preoccupied with the idea of suffering and persecution. Clearly, the recipients of 1 Peter were undergoing very hazardous times, and this may explain why the viewpoint is so very eschatological. The work looks forward all the while, emphasising not so much the present life of the church as its future hope (hope bulks very large in 1 Peter); 'salvation' and 'glory', key concepts in the author's thought, are seen as future realities. The author emphasises that one must rejoice in one's sufferings, which unite one to Christ, but the chief reason for doing so seems to be that present suffering is an assurance of future glory. This eschatological preoccupation makes 1 Peter in some ways a less interesting work than most of the johannine and pauline literature, and its almost military exaltation of the virtue of obedience is a further limitation; that said, it is valuable to see an approach to christianity different in many ways from that of Paul and John (if only because we appreciate Paul and John more after reading 1 Peter!), and at times the author, though incapable of the depth and insight of these two authors, does show a sensitivity that perhaps takes us a bit by surprise. Also, the picture of the condition of the church that we get in 1 Peter helps us to understand why, beset as she was by troubles from without, the church failed either to feel much sense of commitment to society or to work out the implications of the gospel for such social issues as slavery and the subjection of women.

Book list

Apart from the short commentaries in the *Jerusalem Bible and Peake's Commentary* (1962 edition), most of the best works on 1 Peter are rather detailed or technical. The following, though, may be found useful to the general reader:

C. E. B. Cranfield, *I & II Peter, and Jude*, Torch Bible Commentaries, (London 1960).

J. Moffatt, *The General Epistles,—James, Peter and Judas*, Moffatt NT Commentaries, (London 1928).

A. M. Stibbs, *The First Epistle General of Peter*, Tyndale NT Commentaries, (London 1959).

Other works will be found listed in the bibliography in Peake. To Peake's list must now be added, as providing the best treatment of the most vexed text in 1 Peter:

W. J. Dalton, *Christ's Proclamation to the Spirits* (Analecta Biblica, 23), Rome, Pontifical Biblical Institute, 1965.

1

The inheritance and its demands
1 Pet 1:1–2:10

1 Pet 1:1–2

The work begins with a short salutation, expressed in a trinitarian formula, wishing the recipients 'grace and peace' (the combination of these two terms is common in the pauline epistles, but the use of the expression 'be multiplied' is not pauline, but taken from the Greek old testament: Dan 4:1; 6:25 [in some versions 3:98; 4:34]). The author characterises the christian people as a dispersion, or *diaspora* (the word used to denote that part of Jewry living in exile outside the land of Palestine) and as 'aliens and exiles' (cf 2:11): the same idea is found at the beginning of the epistle of James—'James . . . to the twelve tribes in the dispersion: Greeting'. 1 Peter is addressed to people to whom persecution was either a present reality or at least an acute threat, people who must have felt anything but 'at home' in the Roman empire in which they lived, and the concept of the church as the people of God sitting, so to say, in exile beneath the willows of Babylon and ruefully yearning for their homeland and deliverance from the hand of the oppressor, was very apt. It is the perennial position of the church to be a band of 'strangers and exiles on the earth, [who] . . . desire a better country' (Heb 11:13–16, a chapter which provides the most extensive treatment in the new testament of this idea): indeed, our word 'parish' literally means a place of exile (Latin *parochia,* Greek *paroikia*). A sense of exile is part of the judeo-christian heritage, a feeling that should bind Jew and christian together: both can feel the poignancy of the three old testament texts that 1 Peter is alluding to in its use of the expression 'exiles' (1 : 1) and 'aliens and exiles' (2 : 11): 'And Abraham . . . said to the Hittites, I am a stranger and a sojourner among you' (Gen 23 : 3–4. Abraham, our common father, is, of course, the biblical paradigm case of a sojourner); 'I am thy passing guest, a sojourner like all my fathers' (Ps 39 : 12); and '[God said:] The land is mine; you are strangers and sojourners with me' (Lev 25 : 23).

'For obedience to Jesus Christ and for sprinkling with his blood'. In this phrase we must surely detect an allusion to Ex 24 : 7–8, where the combination of the idea of obedience and the sprinkling of blood is also found: '[the people] said, All that the Lord has spoken we will do, and we will be obedient. And Moses took the blood and threw it upon the people and said: Behold the blood of the covenant which the Lord has made with you.' The blood of Jesus does not merely take away sin, it creates, as did the blood sprinkled over the people by Moses, a covenantal community. The Jews, like other ancient peoples, had a strong sense that the life of living things was somehow located in the blood (cf Lev 17/11: 'the life of the flesh is in the blood'), so that to sprinkle the people with blood was to impart to them all a common life. The blood of Christ shed on the cross and given to believers at the eucharist welds them into a covenant people under God, obedient to 'all that the Lord has spoken'.

Are we conscious, when we communicate, that Christ's body and blood welds us into a covenant people under God? And what does this mean?

1 Pet 1:3–12

This solemn and eloquent passage introduces us to the drift of the whole work. The christian is one who has been born to a new life by the resurrection of Christ, but just as the risen Christ has not yet been fully manifested as such (1:7), so our new life, our risen life in him, is for the present only partial: we have still to undergo the 'sufferings' of Christ before we can fully attain to the 'glory' of Christ. Our proper attitude to life is thus a mixture of loving, joyful gratitude for the grace of rebirth and a hopeful longing for our deliverance from the present sorrow which we are given strength to endure through the knowledge that it is sent as a test of our faith and that it gives assurance of future glory.

Note that in 1:11 the author seems to think of the old testament prophets as mouthpieces of the pre-existent Christ. St Paul in 1 Cor 10:4 ('. . . the Rock was Christ') also seems to think of the eternal Son as already in old testament times intervening in human history. A. T. Hanson (*Jesus Christ in the Old Testament*, London 1965) has argued that the same idea is common in the new testament.

'The sufferings of Christ' (1:11), literally 'the sufferings in/unto Christ', perhaps meaning, as F. L. Cross suggests, the sufferings of the church in Christ. This would certainly fit the context better. The gist would then be: 'Your sufferings are no cause for surprise: why, the prophets of old foresaw that anguish and sufferings must precede the final revelation of God's victory (eg,

Joel 2), by which they meant that we christians must, in Christ, suffer now awhile until the day of deliverance dawns.'

'Things into which angels long to look' (1:12). The idea here is probably not that fallen or evil spirits cast longing eyes upon the christian salvation (to which, to judge from other new testament texts, their attitude would be one of fierce hostility rather than pathetic interest), but, as A. T. Hanson says, that the new testament covenant is different from the old testament one in that it is not mediated as that one was by angels: 'the dispensation of which Christ speaks is to be direct, unmediated, an incarnation'. The angels have no part in this covenant, and can only look at it from afar. Man may be 'a little lower than the angels' (Heb 2:7—but the text can also be read as saying that man is for a little *time* lower than the angels), but our relation to, our incorporation in, Christ is a privilege that even angels cannot share: it is our unique privilege as men, made possible precisely because we are bodily creatures. Modern exegetes have put us much in their debt by their rediscovery of the riches of the new testament conception of the human body (see especially John Robinson's book, *The Body*).

1. 'Born anew through the resurrection of Jesus Christ' (1:3). Constantly the new testament speaks of the resurrection where in recent centuries we would have tended to speak of the crucifixion. Are we alive to the significance of the resurrection?

2. Suffering is sent to try us. But is that the end of the story? Are there other insights into the meaning of suffering to be found elsewhere in scripture, which we must place side by side with this? Is any final solution to be found?

1 Pet 1:13–21

If we view 1 Peter as a baptismal homily, we shall probably see in this passage a number of references to the
exodus as a type of baptism: 'gird up your minds' we
shall see as an echo of Ex 12, where the Israelites are told
to eat the paschal lamb with loins girt; 'the precious
blood of Christ, like that of a lamb without blemish or
spot' we shall again see as a reference to the paschal lamb
('your lamb shall be without blemish', Ex 12:5); and we
may see as a further reference to the exodus the quotation
in 1:16 of the words of Lev 11:44: 'Be holy . . . for I am
the Lord *who brought you up out of Egypt,* to be your
God; you shall therefore be holy, for I am holy.' If these
allusions were at the back of our author's mind, their
implications for his thought can be worked out thus: our
christian life is a sort of exodus, a journey in haste with
loins girt through the Red Sea of baptism to the promised
land; this journey is made possible for us by our deliverance through the shedding of the blood of Christ,
our passover lamb; and we are called to holiness of life,
as were the Israelites of old, precisely *because* of this
deliverance.

Even if 1 Peter is not a baptismal homily (or liturgy)
these exodus motifs may be intended, but less certainly,
I think. 'As obedient children' (1:14). Again the idea
of obedience, which we encountered in 1:2. C. Bigg,
comparing 1 Peter with the pauline epistles, has neatly
and illuminatingly characterised Paul's view of christianity as the more *mystical* and 1 Peter's, like James's,
as the more *disciplinarian.* The point of the distinction

may best be brought out in a quotation from Bigg's commentary: 'A Disciplinarian is one who hears God speaking to him; a Mystic is one who feels the presence of God within. The former says, "Christ is my Saviour, Shepherd, Friend, my Judge, my Rewarder"; the latter says, "Not I live, but Christ liveth in me" . . . The leading Disciplinarian ideas are Grace considered as a gift, Law, Learning, Continuity, Godly Fear—in all these human responsibility is kept steadily in view. But the leading Mystic ideas are Grace as an indwelling power, Freedom, the Inner Light, Discontinuity (Law and Gospel, Flesh and Spirit, World and God), and Love.' Such a distinction is useful (though it must not be overworked), and helps us to express the difference in atmosphere which we may sense between 1 Peter and the pauline or johannine writings. These two ways of seeing the one truth, the disciplinarian and the mystic, have often come into conflict in christian history with tragic consequences. Catholics on the whole have inclined much too exclusively in recent centuries to the disciplinarian view, which needs to be supplemented by the more mystic, more prophetic, vision. On the other hand, others have sometimes overlooked the fact that a dsiciplinarian view has a strong basis in scripture, in 1 Peter and James, and, though less exalted than the other conception, it is surely arguable that it needs to be taken account of and that it has and will continue to have an important part to play in the life of the church.

'The futile ways inherited from your fathers' (1:18). This doubtless refers to gentile, not Jewish, ancestors (the recipients of 1 Peter appear to have been mainly gentiles: cf 1:14; 2:10; 4:3–4). In no passage of the new testament do we find any suggestion that pagan religion contained anything but vanity and foolishness. Pagans might indeed (Rom 2:14) live acceptably in the sight of God, but not by virtue of their religion itself, which, being based on idol-worship, was considered a gross 'deceit'. (We may compare the way in which some christians have in more recent times tended to say that christians of other communions than their own could indeed be saved, not through membership of their own church, but almost in spite of it.) It would be absurd not to suppose that we have since obtained insights on this question denied to the age of the apostles or, to put it another way, have drawn out implications from revelation which they did not see to draw.

1. Today we think that buddhists, say, or moslems, can be saved not in spite of their religion but, in part at least, in virtue of it (though still, in some sense, through Christ). In such circumstances, what is the future of missionary zeal?

2. Are the 'disciplinarian' and 'mystical' points of view reconcilable?

1 Pet 1:22–2:10

The exponents of the baptismal homily/liturgy theory tend to posit the administration of the baptism itself between 1:21 and 22, so that 'having purified your souls' and 'you have been born anew' are seen as referring to the immediately preceding act of baptism, and the word of the Lord which is 'the good news that has been preached to you' is taken as referring to the actual words of the rite.

In 1:23–25 two ideas have got closely linked together: (1) God has sent forth his creative word, as at the original creation of the world, and through this word has recreated man: the gospel has been preached to men, and they have been reborn (the moments of conversion and of baptism not being distinguished); (2) God, the sower in the gospel parable, went out to sow: his seed-ground is the world of men, and 'the seed is the word of God' (Lk 8: 11), a seed which will not shrivel up or die, but is imperishable.

'Like new-born babes . . .' (2: 2). The idea here is that since we have been reborn we must imitate the innocence of new-born babes and, putting aside all guile (*dolos*) must long for spiritual milk which is *adolon*, ie guileless, unadulterated.

'You are . . . a holy priesthood, to offer up spiritual sacrifices' (2: 5). It is the whole church which is here considered as a priesthood, not a clerical elite, and the sacrifice that they offer is doubtless the dedication of their whole lives to God, rather than anything as specific as the eucharist—as parallel texts show (eg Rom 12: 1: 'I appeal to you . . . to present your bodies as a living sacrifice, holy and acceptable to God, which is your spiritual worship'). Beare says, on this text, 'The thought of any Christian rite as a sacrifice is foreign to the New Testament'. This seems to me very true, and I think it profoundly regrettable that later christian times saw fit to reverse the rejection by the apostolic age of the opportunity of describing the christian eucharist and ministry in terms of the pagan and old testament ideas of sacrifice and priesthood. This is not at all to deny the validity of the substance of the classical conciliar teachings on these subjects, only to deplore the imagery and concepts in which schoolmen and council fathers elected to express them. The new testament never speaks of the ministry as a priesthood (only the whole church, as in this present passage) nor of the eucharist as a sacrifice (only the total dedication of the christian community to God; this is effected, of course, chiefly through the eucharist). Words, like passions, are good servants but bad masters, and the slavish adherence to the idea of the mass as a sacrifice led in the middle ages, and later, to a mechanical view of its efficacy and a deeply unfortunate neglect of the importance of holy communion, whereas the idea of the clergy as a neo-levitical priesthood made for a playing down of the role of the laity in the church. The obstinate clinging to these terms has also been a constant stumbling block to the reformed churches. How often have words, which are essentially a mode of communication, in fact become barriers to intelligibility and a cause of confusion both to those who hear them and those who utter them!

1. The idea of the preached word as a sort of sacramental force has been neglected in much christian thinking. What are its implications?

2. How can we take all this talk of 'royal priesthood' and 'holy nation' seriously without getting an elite complex?

2

The obligations of a christian
1 Pet 2:11–3:22

1 Pet 2:11–25
Our author here works out the implications of the christian ethic in terms of his disciplinarian view of religion.
The greatest virtue is subordination, to slave-masters, to
magistrates, to the emperor, to God. He does not tell us,
as Paul does (Rom 13), that the reason we must practise
obedience to human institutions is that all authority is
God-given: he merely says, without further rationalisa-
tion, that God requires this obedience of us (2:15). 1
Peter's ethic is perhaps rather incomplete, but what does
come over very strongly in his account is the beauty of
the virtues of humility and patience. 1 Peter presupposes
that the christian will be continually living in an atmosphere of back-biting, misunderstanding, and persecution: in such a situation he has little opportunity to
reform society or to preach a crusade for social justice;
his chief way of influencing his contemporaries is by
'good works' (2:15) and patience, following in the foot-
steps of Christ himself (2:21 ff). It is true that today also
a by no means insignificant proportion of christians are
living in much the same situation as the recipients of 1
Peter, and their christian witness is therefore similarly cir-
cumscribed in scope; but it would be ludicrous to con-
clude that the rest of us have any right to be content with

this ethic: we, because we have the opportunity, have the duty too of taking a full and constructive part in society.

1. What attitude do we have to secular authority?

2. If both responses are possible, is it 'more christian' to endure injustices patiently, or to speak out against injustice and to try to remove its cause?

1 Pet 3:1–7

We come to 1 Peter's ethic of married life. Note the assumption in the text that the christian women were mostly married to pagan husbands, whereas the christian husbands are presumed to have christian wives—it would probably be easier at that time for a man to bring his wife into the church than vice versa. Note too that the wives get six verses, the husbands only one, perhaps because there were more women in the early christian communities than men.

The whole passage breathes the same disciplinarian spirit that we have already encountered elsewhere. The wife is the 'weaker sex' (one would like to be sure that the author means in a physical sense only) and she must subordinate herself to her husband: indeed, the exhortation to respectful obedience to their husbands is the only advice that the writer has to offer women in respect of married life. A rather less severe tone is found in the phrase 'joint heirs of the grace of life' in 3:7, but it remains true that after reading 1 Peter on marriage it is with relief that we turn to the more 'mystical' view of Ephesians.

Is there any sense in which we could today accept that wives should be submissive to their husbands, but not husbands to their wives?

1 Pet 3:8–22

This passage, which begins easily enough with a recapitulation of the praise of good works, patience, and meekness, ends with a section (3:18–22) which is one of the most difficult in the new testament.

In recent centuries the 'traditional' interpretation of this passage has been that it refers to Christ's descent in his soul to Hades after his death, when he liberated men who in the age of Noah had been disobedient. The main objections to this view are: (*a*) 'in his spirit' cannot, according to new testament linguistic usage, mean 'in his disembodied soul'; (*b*) 'spirits' without further qualification never means men, but angelic beings; (*c*) how could Christ liberate the notorious generation of the flood (unless they had repented—and the idea of repentance after death is unscriptural, while the suggestion that they repented before their death is quite gratuitous and unsupported in scripture or Jewish tradition)? Furthermore, though the early church certainly believed in the 'descent into Hades', it never quoted this text in support of this doctrine.

I have no doubt that the correct interpretation is that offered by W. J. Dalton and others. 'Made alive in the spirit' (3:18) refers to Christ's bodily resurrection; 'in which he went' in 3:19 refers to the same event as 'who has gone' in 3:22, ie not the descent to hell but the ascension into heaven; and 'preached to the spirits in prison' (3:19) means that Christ, at the time of his ascension, preached a message, not of liberty, but of defeat to hostile angelic forces. Thus 'he went and preached to the spirits in prison' is exactly equivalent in meaning to the words (in 3:22): 'who has gone into heaven . . . with angels, authorities, and powers subject to him'.

The Jewish apocryphal book called 1 Enoch, which we have long known to have influenced the authors of 2 Peter and Jude, shows us the traditional picture in terms of which we must understand this passage. In the time of Noah angels came down on earth and had sexual relations with women (see Gen 6): this was, as Genesis makes clear, the reason for God's sending the flood. 1 Enoch recounts how God sent Enoch to go (*poreuein*—the same word as in 1 Pet 3:19, 22) to these wicked spirits and announce to them that they would remain in eternal imprisonment for their sins in a prison-house among the stars. Christ in 1 Peter is seen as repeating Enoch's errand; by announcing, at the time of his ascension heavenwards, the eternal subjugation of these angels imprisoned in the sky he emphasises his conquest of evil (one school of Jewish thought represented these disobedient spirits as the source of all human ills). The reason why 1 Peter refers to this definitive victory of Christ over evil is to comfort the christians of Asia in their sufferings. (The descent into Hades interpretation, incidentally, would have no relevance to the context at all.)

'The pledge of a good conscience' (3:21), if that is the correct rendering (all others seem very unsatisfactory) refers to the promises which one makes at one's baptism, whereby, as it were, one pledges oneself to maintain a good conscience.

Can we take seriously the world of spirits, good and bad, which we find in the new testament, or are we somehow to 'demythologise' it?

3

The end is at hand
1 Pet 4:1–11

1 Pet 4:1–6

1 Pet 4:6 is also often taken as a reference to the descent
into Hades, but most implausibly. It probably refers to
those christians who had died since receiving the gospel
message. This fits the context very well: our author is still
trying to persuade christian victims of persecution that
their sufferings are worth while, so he says that even if
some have been put to death since having the gospel
preached to them their sufferings were not in vain, for
'though they were condemned by men, in the flesh, they
are alive to God in the spirit.'

In 4:1 the phrase 'whoever has suffered in the flesh
has ceased from sin' has puzzled commentators. A brilli-
ant, if unproved, suggestion has been offered by F. L.
Cross. He points out that some church fathers, and perhaps even Philo before them, treated the word *pasch* as
being cognate with the Greek verb *paschein*, 'to suffer'
(wrongly, of course, but that is beside the point), and
Cross thinks that 1 Peter may also be thinking of the
passover and suffering as having this etymological connection: the pasch takes its name from suffering, and
all suffering is paschal, so that the man who has suffered
in the flesh has undergone a paschal experience and is
associated with the paschal event of Christ, so that having

suffered in Christ he is now risen also in Christ and therefore lives now in a resurrection life where sin has no
place (cf Rom 6 : 8, 11: 'if we have died with Christ, we
believe that we shall also live with him . . . so you also
must consider yourselves dead to sin and alive to God in
Christ Jesus').

*What does it mean to say that we live now in a resur-
rection life? What does it mean to say that sin has no
place in this life?*

1 Pet 4:7–11

The urgent sense of this paragraph surely belies the
judgement of those who make too much of the difference
in tone between the first half of 1 Peter and the second
half (ie 4 : 12 ff), treating the former as calm, quiet, and
level-spirited, the latter as staccato, anxious, and urgent.
'The end of all things is at hand' (4 : 7): therefore christians must become acutely conscious of their primary
duty as 'good stewards of the grace of God in its varied
forms'. The uncertainty of things, and the ever-present
fear of the police, inevitably persuaded the first-century
christians that the second coming could not be long de-
layed. We may no longer have occasion to expect an imminent parousia, but the sense of urgency is surely part
of the permanent christian heritage; if torture and execution are not an immediate danger, the misery and god-
lessness of our contemporaries, the tragedy and scandal
of christian disunity, must keep us on our toes. If the
author of 1 Peter were writing today, his tone surely
would be no less insistent or apostolic: our own comfort
and prosperity are, he would say, no excuse for complac-
ency in the face of wholesale christian persecution in

eastern Europe, in the face of tragic warfare in Asia, of racial oppression in Africa, of a degree of world famine which is a standing condemnation of and challenge to the christian conscience. Note the exhortation to 'practise hospitality ungrudgingly to one another' (4:9). The christian ministers were poor men who could not afford to put up at inns, so they depended on the hospitality of the faithful. The fact that the latter needed to be reminded to be hospitable (cf Heb 13:2; 3 Jn 5–8) is revealing. Not that the fault was all on one side—it would seem that the clergy tended to presume on hospitality, for we find the *Didache* (first or second century) having to restrict the time for which an evangelist was allowed to impose himself upon his hosts: 'Let every apostle that comes to you be received as the Lord; and he shall stay but one day, and, if need be, the next day also; but if he stay three days he is a false prophet. When the apostle goes forth, let him take nothing but bread to suffice till he reach his lodging; if he ask for money he is a false prophet.' 1 Pet 5:2 probably indicates that some of the elders had already been behaving in a mercenary way. The early christians often seem uncomfortably like ourselves, despite our desire to be able to look back upon a golden age of christianity when generosity came naturally and virtue was easy!

1. Is a sense of urgency necessary if people are to behave responsibly?

2. Is it a relief or a disappointment to discover that even the christians of the apostolic age shared many of our own weaknesses?

4

The necessity of suffering
1 Pet 4:12–5:14

1 Pet 4:12–19

The second half of 1 Peter begins with a warning against surprise at persecution ('trial by fire', *pyrosis,* probably refers to the idea of gold being refined by fire—cf 1 : 7 —not to the idea of burning at the stake); suffering, our author says, is sent to try us, and it involves us in a fellowship with Christ: as he suffered and was later glorified, so we know that if we suffer now we shall in the future be glorified; already 'the spirit of glory and of God rests upon' (4 : 14) us. *Glory* is, of course, in the old testament a technical word for the quasi-visible presence of God (later called the *Shekinah*) which filled the tent of meeting, and afterwards the holy of holies in the temple, and the word often carries overtones of this meaning in the new testament. Certainly these overtones would seem to be present in this present passage, for our author twice refers to the church as the temple of God ('like living stones be yourselves built into a spiritual house', 2 : 5; 'For the time has come for judgement to begin with the household of God', 4 : 17). It is no longer in temples made with hands that the presence of the Lord dwells, but in the temple of the body of Christ, both in the sense of his personal body and his church-body. We are not just individuals in either our sufferings or our

glorification: it is in Christ that our sufferings have meaning, and in Christ too that we shall be glorified. Already
the glory is present in Christ, and already it rests upon
the church as the new temple of God, but we as individuals have not yet attained glorification, but look forward
constantly to attaining it through our fellowship in
Christ and our imitation of him (the idea of the imitation
of Christ clearly lies behind the exhortation of the hearers
of the letter to 'entrust their souls to a faithful Creator',
4 : 19; cf Christ's 'into thy hands I commend my spirit').

The idea of judgement beginning at the house of God
is an allusion to Ezek 9 : 6. Ezekiel had just seen the glory
depart from the temple (whither it never came back) and
the Lord turned his anger against all the people except
'the men who sigh and groan over all the abominations
that are committed in Jerusalem' (Ezek 9 : 4), *beginning
at the sanctuary*, that is, with the men most closely con-
nected with the performance of the cultus, for they had
the least excuse for their sins. It seems possible that the
reason that 1 Peter immediately goes on (Chapter 5) to
counsel 'the elders' in the christian church is that he, like
Ezekiel, thinks of the ministers of God as having most to
answer for: the glory has returned, and has come to rest
over Christ and his holy house, so woe betide those who
allow the sins of Israel of old to be repeated, especially
those who are given responsibility over the church. However, as we have seen, the new testament nowhere treats
the christian ministry as the counterpart of the old testament priesthood—the new testament priests are the whole
people of God—so it is probable that 'beginning at the
House of God' means for 1 Peter not beginning at the
clergy, as distinct from the laity, but beginning at the
church, as distinct from those outside it: we christians are

the first to suffer because on us the greatest gifts have
been lavished: cf the thought of Amos 3:2:

> You only have I known,
>   of all the families of earth;
> Therefore will I punish you,
>   for all your iniquities.

*We can understand how suffering unites us to Christ.
But how does it cause 'the spirit of glory and of God' to
rest upon us?*

1 Pet 5:1–14

This last chapter begins with an exhortation to the elders
(the word clearly refers to an office in the church, but the
original idea of seniority of years is still partly present,
as may be seen from the contrast with 'you that are
younger' 5:5) not to misuse their authority. What we
have called the disciplinarian spirit of 1 Peter is very
much in evidence in this chapter; but even within this
rather stern view of authority in the church, a christian
tenderness can still breathe, as in the counsel to 'clothe
yourselves . . . with humility toward one another' (5:5)
and to 'cast all your anxieties on him (God) for he cares
about you' (5:7).

'. . . a fellow elder and a witness of the sufferings of
Christ, as well as a partaker in the glory that is to be
revealed' (5:1). Our anonymous author, writing, as it
were, in the person of Peter (his purpose in doing this is
perhaps to try to mediate to the persecuted churches of
Asia the message which he thought the prince of the
apostles would have wished to send them) here attempts
to raise the spirits of the faithful and to assure them that
the glory which lies in the future is as certain as the

sufferings that they are undergoing in the present, by reminding them that Peter himself as surely witnessed the
glory of Christ at the transfiguration as he did his sufferings on Calvary.

'Your adversary the devil prowls around like a roaring
lion, seeking someone to devour. Resist him . . . the same
experience of suffering is required of your brotherhood
throughout the world' (5:8–9). The thought here is a
little confused: the devil is called an 'adversary' (*anti-
dikos* = prosecution counsel) because the author is thinking of the devil as responsible for accusations brought
against christians in the law-courts; but when such accusations come, provided they are not false accusations (eg
of murder, theft, or civil disturbance: 4:15) his teaching
is not that they should be resisted but that we must give
a defence of the hope that is in us (3:15) and rejoice if
we are punished as christians (4:16). However, the author
is probably also thinking of the devil in more general
terms, not merely as the cause of suffering through legal
actions, but as a foe and a tempter, as which he is always
to be vigorously resisted.

*1. Are there any insights, gained from elsewhere in the
new testament, into the nature of authority in the church
with which we should wish to supplement 1 Peter's
outlook?*

*2. Is expectation of the glory an idea which can mean
something to us today? Or must we rephrase or reformu-
late the christian hope as seen by 1 Peter?*